CLASSIC
MATCHES

YORKSHIRE
COUNTY CRICKET CLUB

STADIA

CLASSIC
MATCHES

YORKSHIRE
COUNTY CRICKET CLUB

MICK POPE AND PAUL DYSON

STADIA

Acknowledgements

We are most grateful to Tempus Publishing, and especially James Howarth, for allowing us to contribute this volume to their Classic Matches series.

In addition we are grateful to Tracy Pope for her proofreading, computer work and scanning, Willie Sugg in connection with the Cambridgeshire game, Worcestershire CCC, Cricket Archive, Peter Wynne-Thomas, archivist, Nottinghamshire CCC and the staff at Leeds Central Library.

We are most grateful to the following for the use of photographs: Andrew Hignell, Andrew Johnson, Roger Mann, Paul McGregor, Steve Sheen and David Williams.

Paul Dyson, Easingwold, York
Mick Pope, Scholes, Rotherham
March 2007

First published 2007

STADIA is an imprint of
Tempus Publishing Limited
The Mill, Brimscombe Port,
Stroud, Gloucestershire, GL5 2QG
www.tempus-publishing.com

© Mick Pope and Paul Dyson, 2007

British Library Cataloguing in Publication Data.
A catalogue record for this book is available from the British Library.

ISBN 978 0 7524 3787 3

Typesetting and origination by Tempus Publishing Limited.
Printed in Great Britain.

Introduction

Choosing fifty of Yorkshire's most significant matches was never going to be an easy task. The selection comes from a grand total (to the end of the 2006 season) of 3,429 first-class matches and 778 competitive limited-overs games.

A team calling itself 'Yorkshire' took the field for the first time in 1833, at Sheffield against Norfolk, and this fixture begins our selection. Yorkshire CCC was formed in 1863 and its first game – against Surrey at The Oval – is also included. We have also chosen the following:

1) First-class matches (43):
a. The three first-class games that were all won in one day;
b. The game which had Yorkshire's biggest win;
c. The two games that ended in ties;
d. The only game that Yorkshire have ever won by one run;
e. The game that featured Yorkshire's highest fourth innings-winning total;
f. The two (out of five) most emphatic victories gained after having followed on;
g. The four games that involved Yorkshire bowlers taking all ten wickets in an innings;
h. The two games that featured Yorkshire players scoring their 100th centuries;
i. The two games that featured Yorkshire's highest partnerships for the first wicket;
j. The games that featured Yorkshire's highest total and the lowest total against Yorkshire;
k. The games that featured the highest individual innings and the best match bowling analysis;
l. The game that featured an individual scoring two centuries and taking ten wickets;
m. A total of eighteen personal choices of games which each have their own special story.

2) Limited-overs matches (7):
a. The four cup finals which Yorkshire have won;
b. The game which contained the highest individual innings;
c. Two personal choices.

As the book takes in the entire 175-year span of county cricket in Yorkshire it acts as a microcosm of its story – its Championship successes and its great players as well as some of its days of disappointment.

The 50 Classic Matches

1833	v. Norfolk	Hyde Park, Sheffield
1863	v. Surrey	The Oval
1867	v. Cambridgeshire	Wisbech, Cambridgeshire
1889	v. Surrey	The Oval
1894	v. Somerset	Huddersfield
1896	v. Warwickshire	Edgbaston
1898	v. Hampshire	Southampton
1898	v. Derbyshire	Chesterfield
1900	v. Worcestershire	Bradford
1901	v. Nottinghamshire	Trent Bridge
1901	v. Somerset	Headingley
1902	v. Australians	Headingley
1905	v. Leicestershire	Aylestone Road, Leicester
1906	v. Somerset	Bath
1914	v. Somerset	Weston-super-Mare
1921	v. Northamptonshire	Harrogate
1922	v. Gloucestershire	Bristol
1925	v. Sussex	Bradford
1931	v. Warwickshire	Headingley
1932	v. Essex	Leyton
1932	v. Gloucestershire	Bradford
1932	v. Nottinghamshire	Headingley
1933	v. Essex	Leyton
1939	v. Derbyshire	Bramall Lane, Sheffield
1939	v. Sussex	Hove
1951	v. Somerset	Bramall Lane, Sheffield
1951	v. Surrey	The Oval
1952	v. Lancashire	Old Trafford
1954	v. Leicestershire	Huddersfield
1957	v. Worcestershire	Worcester
1959	v. Sussex	Hove
1959	v. The Rest of England	The Oval
1961	v. Worcestershire	Worcester
1962	v. Hampshire	Bradford
1963	v. West Indians	Middlesbrough
1965	v. Surrey	Lord's
1967	v. Gloucestershire	Harrogate
1968	v. Australians	Bramall Lane, Sheffield

1969	v. Derbyshire	Lord's
1973	v. Middlesex	Bradford
1976	v. Middlesex	Bradford
1982	v. Warwickshire	Edgbaston
1987	v. Northamptonshire	Lord's
1995	v. Lancashire	Headingley
1996	v. Lancashire	Old Trafford
1996	v. Essex	Headingley
2001	v. Lancashire	Headingley
2001	v. Nottinghamshire	Scarborough
2002	v. Somerset	Lord's
2005	v. Leicestershire	Grace Road, Leicester

STATISTICAL NOTES

In the scorecards the following apply:

* = Captain

+ = Wicketkeeper

Second innings batting order (where known) is indicated when different from the first innings by the figures in brackets.

Yorkshire captain Richard Blakey and the team celebrate their victory over Somerset at Lord's in the 2002 C&G Trophy final.

YORKSHIRE v. NORFOLK

Date: 2, 3, 4, 5 September 1833   Unofficial inter-county
Location: Hyde Park, Sheffield

This fixture would, in due course, be recognised by cricket historians as Yorkshire's first-ever 'county' match, although the home side were in effect a 'Sheffield' XI under a different title. The game took place at the Hyde Park ground (opened in 1826 by Messrs Wright and Hazelhurst) which, under the management of William Woolhouse (who opened the batting for Yorkshire), had established itself as the city's major cricket venue in succession to Darnall. The ground took almost two years to complete and cost in excess of £4,000 – a huge amount at the time. The opposition – Norfolk – included in their ranks Fuller Pilch, the premier batsman in England during the 1830s. Pilch, a middle-order right-hand batsman and slow round-arm bowler, had comprehensively defeated Sheffield's leading cricketer Tom Marsden in a single-wicket encounter (also at Hyde Park) just a month before the 'county' game by 127 runs. Two of Pilch's brothers – William and Nathaniel – also lined up in the Norfolk side! As well as Marsden, 'Yorkshire' included in their ranks three 'gentlemen' players, as the local newspaper thus described them, denoted by Esq. in their scorecard. They were W. Lupton, P.S. Johnston and Thomas Barker, a native of Bakewell, Derbyshire, who would later, in 1848, serve as mayor of Sheffield. The young Barker was a more-than-useful left-arm round-arm bowler.

Yorkshire, having won the toss, mustered 138 in their first innings with the left-handed opening batsman Woolhouse top-scoring. The local hero, Marsden, 'appeared full of spirit and confidence, and bent on mischief', but was bowled second ball for nought, much to the disappointment of the Sheffield spectators. By the close of play, Norfolk had been dismissed for a meagre 67, Fuller Pilch making just 10. That was certainly noted by the local Sheffield scribe who wrote, 'The backers of the Norfolk men now looked blue.'

Poor weather on the second day (Tuesday) meant that play didn't resume until around three o'clock. The rain returned after an hour's play and Yorkshire closed on 39 for 2 in their second innings having lost Deakin and Lupton. Although cold and showery on day three, the weather was kinder. James Dearman, having been promoted in the order, took his score to 40 before he was dismissed. The 'Sheffield Champion'

Hyde Park cricket ground, Sheffield – venue for Yorkshire's first county match.

Marsden, determined to atone for his first-innings failure and with a point to prove particularly to Pilch, lifted his side's total to 196, leaving Norfolk to face a daunting victory target of 268. Marsden's innings of 53 was the highest score in the match and the only 50 registered by both sides. 'His batting was excellent – bold, yet steady and careful,' read the proud newspaper report in *The Sheffield & Rotherham Advertiser*. It took a ball from his old antagonist Pilch to remove him. By the end of Wednesday's play the match was effectively over: Norfolk were 86 for 5, which included Fuller Pilch amongst the wickets to have fallen. The remaining Norfolk batsmen were finally disposed of on the fourth day (Thursday) to leave Yorkshire victorious by the margin of 120 runs. This first 'historic' county match for the White Rose was not a close or tense encounter and it was to be a further thirty years before an 'official' County Club became a reality.

YORKSHIRE v. NORFOLK

Yorkshire won the toss and elected to bat.

Umpires: not known.

YORKSHIRE

W.H. Woolhouse	run out	31	( ) b N. Pilch	13
E. Vincent	b Daplyn	19	(4) c Wilkinson	32
G. Smith	c F. Pilch	19	( ) c Wilkinson	0
T. Marsden	b Daplyn	0	(3) b F. Pilch	53
G.E. Dawson	c Pile	7	b N. Pilch	12
G. Rawlins	c Pile	7	c Pile	6
W. Lupton	b F. Pilch	1	(2) c Pile	0
P.S. Johnson	b F. Pilch	7	b N. Pilch	6
T.R. Barker	b F. Pilch	0	not out	4
J. Dearman	not out	14	(1) c Wilkinson	40
T. Deakin	c Hogg	8	c W. Pilch	11
Extras	(b16 w9)	25	(b13 w4 nb2)	19
TOTAL		138		196

FOW 1st: 61, 10-138
FOW 2nd: 10-196

Bowling 1st: Dalpyn 2w Spinks 0w F. Pilch 3w N. Pilch 0w

Bowling 2nd: F. Pilch 1w N. Pilch 3w

NORFOLK

F. Semmence	b Marsden	3	(3) b Marsden	0
N. Pilch	run out	10	(1) b Dearman	22
M. Daplyn	lbw	5	( ) c Vincent	0
C.A. Wilkinson	b Marsden	5	( ) c Dearman	25
F. Pilch	c Vincent	10	(4) c Vincent	23
A. Spinks	b Marsden	1	not out	14
W. Roberts	c Deakin	0	(2) run out	21
E. Hogg	c Rawlins	1	run out	3
W. Pilch	run out	5	b Rawlins	8
Pile	b Dearman	20	b Marsden	11
Groom	not out	1	c Smith	0
Extras	(b2 w3 nb1)	6	(b10 w9 nb1)	20
TOTAL		67		147

FOW 1st: 10-67
FOW 2nd: 1-3, 10-147

Bowling 1st: Rawlins 0w Marsden 3w Dearman 1w

Bowling 2nd: Rawlins 1w Marsden 2w Dearman 1w

YORKSHIRE WON BY 120 RUNS

SURREY v. YORKSHIRE

Date: 4, 5, 6 June 1863   Official inter-county

Location: The Oval

The team that played in this match was the first to represent Yorkshire in an official capacity. Since the fixture against Norfolk, a further twenty-eight matches had been played by teams purporting to call themselves Yorkshire. However, a meeting at the Adelphi Hotel in Sheffield on 8 January 1863 put an end to this nonsense. Yorkshire County Cricket Club was now formed.

The team that took the field on this momentous occasion was truly representative of the county. Three came from each of Huddersfield and Sheffield, two from Bedale and one from each of Bradford, Ripon and Selby. Two of them – George Anderson and John Berry – had played in the first (unofficial) Yorkshire v. Surrey game twelve years previously.

Yorkshire were led by their first captain, Roger Iddison, who was to remain at the helm for ten seasons, despite spending some time also playing for Lancashire! A powerful all-rounder, he had made his debut in important cricket in 1853 and had been on the first tour to Australia just eighteen months previously. This also applied to the wicketkeeper Edwin Stephenson.

Unfortunately, the match did not live up to the occasion, especially in terms of the weather, all three days being affected. This was less so on the first day when, after a 12.15p.m. start, Surrey made a first innings score of 315 and the visitors ended, at 7.30p.m., on 12 for 0. The hosts' first four wickets were all taken by Isaac Hodgson and although William Mortlock lasted for about two hours, wickets fell at regular intervals, the highest partnership being 51 for the sixth wicket. The last four wickets were taken by Berry who then proceeded to open the batting with John Thewlis snr (not to be confused with his nephew, a later Yorkshire player with the same name), the experienced pair's combined ages adding up to seventy-five.

Day two was the least interesting of the three, play not starting until 4.30p.m. and lasting for only two hours, Yorkshire taking their first-innings score on to 143 for 5. As in Surrey's innings, the bowlers were very much on top with William Caffyn and George Whale being entrusted to bowl 64% of the overs and the overall run rate was a paltry 1.8 runs per over. By close of play, Ned Stephenson had taken his score to 39 and he had just been joined by Anderson. This pair held Surrey up for a while on the final day but, after both had been dismissed, the last four wickets fell for just 19 runs and Surrey had a lead of 58.

An extract from the minutes of the committee meeting held at the Adelphi Hotel in January 1863 that recorded: '...this Committee undertake to get up a home match between Surrey and Yorkshire to be played at the Oval on the 4th June and then on the 27th July ...' The minutes further resolved to form a County Club and thus the match against Surrey at The Oval became Yorkshire CCC's first official first-class match.

SURREY v. YORKSHIRE

As there was little time for a result, the home side decided to rearrange its batting order but this was a fateful decision. The skipper was soon dismissed by Hodgson whereupon his partner, William Slinn, took all of the next four wickets and Surrey collapsed to 38 for 6. Only Mortlock, top-scoring for the second time in the match, put up much resistance. The pair bowled throughout the whole of Surrey's innings and the home side was all out for 60 but it had taken them 52 overs.

With 119 required for victory, an interesting duel would have taken place on a difficult pitch, but it was not to be and the game ended as a draw. At the end of July, the return game took place at Bramall Lane, Sheffield and the home side won a see-saw tussle by three wickets. Meanwhile, Yorkshire had played two games against Nottinghamshire, winning one and losing one. These four matches were the total for the season and a start had been made.

SURREY v. YORKSHIRE

Surrey won the toss and elected to bat

Umpires: W. Cuttell and G. Lee

SURREY

W. Mortlock	c&b Hodgson	72	(7) st Stephenson b Slinn	17
T. Humphrey	c Slinn b Hodgson	18	(3) c Stephenson b Slinn	1
H.H. Stephenson	b Hodgson	11	(8) c Rowbotham b Slinn	6
W. Caffyn	b Hodgson	27	(5) st Stephenson b Slinn	0
G. Griffith	c Thewlis b Slinn	61	(6) c Thewlis b Hodgson	3
Mr E. Dowson	b Slinn	45	(9) st Stephenson b Hodgson	0
J. Caesar	b Berry	28	(4) b Slinn	11
T. Lockyer+	not out	26	(2) b Hodgson	6
Mr F.P. Miller*	c Atkinson b Berry	8	(1) b Hodgson	13
T. Sewell jun	c Rowbotham b Berry	2	not out	0
G. Whale	c Dawson b Berry	1	b Hodgson	0
Extras	(b8 lb8)	16	(b1 lb1 w1)	3
TOTAL		315		60

FOW 1st: 38, 71, 126, 160, 223, 274, 279, 308, ???, 315
FOW 2nd: 15, 16, 34, 34, 35, 38, 59, 60, 60, 60

Bowling 1st: Hodgson 57-17-96-4 Slinn 45-13-83-2 Atkinson 37-13-68-0 Berry 19-8-26-4

Bowling 2nd: Hodgson 26-13-27-5 Slinn 26-14-30-5

YORKSHIRE

John Thewlis	c Mortlock b Whale	17
John Berry	c Griffith b Caffyn	35
J. Rowbotham	c Mortlock b Sewell	27
E. Stephenson+	c Griffith b Miller	67
E. Dawson	hit wkt b Griffith	10
R. Iddison*	c Lockyer b Caffyn	10
G. Anderson	b Whale	46
Mr B.W. Waud	b Griffith	22
G.R. Atkinson	c Mortlock b Whale	6
I. Hodgson	b Griffith	7
W. Slinn	not out	2
Extras	(b1 lb4 w3)	8
TOTAL		257

FOW 1st: 33, 81, 81, 109, 136, 199, 238, 248, 252, 257

Bowling 1st: Caffyn 45-17-72-2 Whale 46-15-94-3 Griffith 14-1-32-3 Sewell 18-7-34-1 Miller 18-6-17-1

MATCH DRAWN

CAMBRIDGESHIRE v. YORKSHIRE

Date: 16, 17 July 1867   Official inter-county

Location: Wisbech, Cambridgeshire

Played against the back-drop of a long-running feud between players from the North and South, this encounter had originally been scheduled for 8 July at Bramall Lane, Sheffield. However, the decision by the Sheffield committee to revive relations with Surrey by staging their match with Yorkshire in June, was the precursor for a certain number of the Cambridge professionals ('out of spite', as it is recorded in *Scores & Biographies*, Vol. 10) to refuse to play at the Sheffield venue. The match was switched to Wisbech and in late July the two sides met again at Dewsbury. Scheduled to start on Monday 15 July, rain prevented any play until the Tuesday.

The Wisbech clash was, despite the off-field disputes, worth the wait. The Northern county, by the close of the 1867 season, would have secured an unbeaten record (played seven, won seven) and, after two disastrous and difficult years in 1865 and 1866, laid claim to the unofficial title of 'Champion County'. The closest Yorkshire came to defeat that summer was in this hard-fought fixture with Cambridgeshire that proved to be the narrowest first-class victory that season.

The major talent in the home XI centred on the batting of Tom Hayward and Robert Carpenter and the fast round-arm bowler George 'Tear 'em' Tarrant. All three had toured Australia in 1863/64 with George Parr's party. Yorkshire matched those with three bowlers of real quality in Tom Emmett (left-hand round-arm fast), George Freeman (right-hand quick) and, from Huddersfield, Luke Greenwood (right-hand round-arm fast). The latter two claimed five wickets apiece and dismissed Cambridgeshire for just 86, before lunch, in their first innings. Only Hayward and Scott, with 18 not out, offered any significant resistance. Tarrant, though,

George Freeman – eight for 60 in the match.

was in equally good form, capturing six Yorkshire victims at a personal cost of only 27 from 31 overs. Sheffield's Joseph Rowbotham, who in later years would captain his county, made the most substantial batting contributions on either side in both innings with scores of 34 (run out) in the first innings and 34 not out in Yorkshire's second-innings run chase of 91 for victory. Rowbotham, or 'Old Tarpot' as he was nicknamed, was a fine punishing right-hand batsman and excellent point and long-stop fieldsman. Tarrant played his part with the bat in Cambridgeshire's second knock, top scoring with 29.

The rest of the home batting offered very little against Freeman (who took his match tally to 8 for 60; he would claim 51 first-class wickets in the season at an average of only 7.45 runs each!) and, this time, Emmett with six wickets. On the second day the game became a personal battle between Tarrant's quick stuff and the solid Rowbotham. The express Cambridgeshire bowler removed the Yorkshire openers: Gideon Holgate for a duck and Emmett for just two. Despite Tarrant's seven second-innings wickets (match figures of 13 wickets for

CAMBRIDGESHIRE v. YORKSHIRE

60 runs), Yorkshire scraped home by one wicket, with Sheffield's Rowbotham unbeaten at the end and last man John Burman (playing in his only first-class match) one not out. It took Yorkshire just over 100 overs to score the required 91 runs. Tarrant's 51.3 overs included 36 maidens.

A match that had started amid controversy had its fair share at the close of the first day with a 'dispute about a decision of the Yorkshire umpire' [Copeland]. The argument was settled at the White Lion and play continued on day two. After two seasons without a single victory the White Rose county were able to complete a season of unprecedented success.

CAMBRIDGESHIRE v. YORKSHIRE

Cambridgeshire won the toss and elected to bat

Umpires: F.W. Bell and Constable/Copeland

CAMBRIDGESHIRE

C. Warren	b Freeman	1	b Emmett		0
D. Hayward	c Emmett b Greenwood	2	(7) run out		3
John Smith	c Rawlinson b Greenwood	5	(2) c Stephenson b Emmett		9
T. Hayward	b Greenwood	27	c Greenwood b Emmett		2
R. Carpenter	b Freeman	9	(3) b Freeman		4
G. Tarrant	lbw b Freeman	11	b Freeman		29
J.H. Marshall	c Freeman b Greenwood	4	(8) b Emmett		2
F.C. Pryor	b Greenwood	0	(9) not out		7
A.T. Scott	not out	18	c Anderson b Emmett		3
E. Cowell	b Freeman	5	b Freeman		8
W. Watts	b Freeman	0	b Emmett		0
Extras	(b1 lb2 w1)	4	(b2 lb4 w1)		7
TOTAL		86			74

FOW 1st: 4, 4, 11, 32, 52, 59, 59, 70, 81, 86
FOW 2nd: 6, 11, 15, 16, 38, 48, 57, 57, 73, 74

Bowling 1st: Freeman 34.2-16-36-5 Greenwood 34-17-46-5

Bowling 2nd: Freeman 18-7-24-3 Emmett 17.2-9-43-6

YORKSHIRE

G. Holgate	c Carpenter b Tarrant	1	(3) b Tarrant		0
T. Emmett	c D. Hayward b Watts	4	(2) b Tarrant		2
E. Stephenson	b Tarrant	13	(1) c Scott b T. Hayward		10
J. Rowbotham	run out	34	(5) not out		34
R. Iddison	c Smith b T. Hayward	6	(4) lbw b Tarrant		11
G. Britton	b Tarrant	0	(9) b Tarrant		3
G. Freeman	b Tarrant	2	b Tarrant		6
E.B. Rawlinson	b Tarrant	1	(10) c Watts b Tarrant		13
L. Greenwood	b Tarrant	4	(8) b Tarrant		2
G. Anderson	not out	2	c Marshall b T. Hayward		1
J. Burman	b T. Hayward	0	(6) not out		1
Extras	(b3)	3	(b4 lb1 w3)		8
TOTAL		70	(9 wkts)		91

FOW 1st: 1, 14, 36, 61, 61, 63, 63, 69, 69, 70
FOW 2nd: 3, 3, 21, 35, 39, 49, 60, 66, 86

Bowling 1st: Tarrant 31-16-27-6 Watts 15-4-21-1 T. Hayward 15.3-7-19-2

Bowling 2nd: Tarrant 51.3-36-33-7 Watts 16-7-20-0 T. Hayward 32.2-11-30-2

It is not certain who captained and kept wicket for both Cambridgeshire and Yorkshire

YORKSHIRE WON BY ONE WICKET

SURREY v. YORKSHIRE

Date: 26, 27 August 1889
Location: The Oval

Official inter-county

Known as the 'Gaslight Match', Yorkshire's two-wicket defeat in the late August darkness was described by Lord Hawke (Yorkshire's then captain) in his *Recollections and Reminiscences*: 'It has been so often written about as to be a classic.' *James Lillywhite's Cricketers' Annual* (Red Lilly) for 1890 referred to the game as 'One of the most remarkable finishes ever witnessed'.

Played on a very wet surface, following heavy rains, Lord Hawke's side batted first and George Ulyett and Louis Hall compiled a useful opening stand of 34 before wickets started to fall with regularity to Surrey's fast bowler John Beaumont. At 71 for 7, Bobby Moorhouse ('who played with great confidence and judgment') was joined by Saul Wade. Together they added a vital 59 for the eighth wicket. By the close of the Yorkshire first innings, both sides were effectively down to ten men. Hawke sustained a bad blow to the hand whilst batting and Surrey's Maurice Read sprained a finger whilst catching the Yorkshire skipper.

Surrey's reply was curtailed by the slow left-arm bowling of Bobby Peel and they ended 24 runs in arrears on first innings. At 73 for 2 in the second innings, with Hall and Fred Lee going well, Yorkshire looked in command of the situation. However, their last eight wickets fell for just a further 68 runs, leaving the home side a victory target of 166 in three and a quarter hours if the match was to be finished inside two days.

No player in three completed innings had yet passed 50 and it seemed likely that would remain the case when Surrey slipped to 43 for 4 in their second-innings run chase. Enter Robert Henderson to partner the amateur Kingsmill Key. The pair added 34 for the fifth wicket before 'the Old Cliftonian threw away his wicket by a foolish call...' Ted Wainwright removed Bill Lockwood and wicketkeeper Henry Wood in quick succession and Surrey were now 105 for 7 with Read unlikely to contribute at no.11. Henderson found some support from John Sharpe but 30 were still needed when a quick ball from Ulyett bowled Sharpe for 14.

When the official time to draw stumps (6.15p.m.) was reached, the home side still required a further 26 runs for victory, Yorkshire probably just one wicket. Both captains agreed that an extra half hour should be played. With the gloomy light fading badly and against tight straight bowling, Henderson and Beaumont

Bobby Moorhouse – a vital first-innings 47 not out and Yorkshire's highest score in the match.

were still 14 runs short of their target when the clock reached 6.45p.m. By that stage the gas-lamps outside The Oval ground were alight and from the boundary the spectators and players could hardly see the ball. Hawke left it to Jack Shuter, the Surrey captain, to consult with Henderson who chose to bat on. Just before seven o'clock Henderson struck the winning runs and left the field amid great excitement and cheering from the almost visionless crowd. He had batted for two and three quarter hours in compiling his chanceless 59 not out, the highest score of the match made, for the most part, in dreary light. By his 'consummate judgment as well as confidence', the Surrey right-hander had secured a victory that would pass into cricket folklore as 'the match that ended in the dark'.

SURREY v. YORKSHIRE

Yorkshire won the toss and elected to bat

Umpires: R. Thoms and R. Carpenter

YORKSHIRE

G. Ulyett	c Shuter b Beaumont	22	(3) b Lohmann		2
L. Hall	b Beaumont	14	b Lohmann		33
F. Lee	b Beaumont	12	(4) b Lockwood		32
R. Peel	c Henderson b Beaumont	2	(5) b Lohmann		22
E. Wainwright	b Beaumont	7	(6) b Lohmann		5
Lord Hawke*	c J.M. Read b Lohmann	7	absent hurt		-
J.T. Brown	c Wood b Beaumont	3	(7) c Wood b Beaumont		10
S. Wade	b Sharpe	23	(1) c W.W. Read b Sharpe		3
R. Moorhouse	not out	47	(8) c Wood b Beaumont		17
L. Whitehead	b Sharpe	0	(9) b Lohmann		2
D. Hunter+	b Sharpe	0	(10) not out		1
Extras	(lb1)	1	(b12 lb1 nb1)		14
TOTAL		138			141

FOW 1st: 34, 40, 52, 55, 58, 66, 71, 130, 130, 138
FOW 2nd: 26, 28, 73, 97, 109, 118, 124, 129, 141

Bowling 1st: Beaumont 30-15-46-6 Lohmann 29-8-68-1 Sharpe 4.3-2-7-3 W.W. Read 1-0-4-0 Abel 2-0-12-0

Bowling 2nd: Beaumont 22.2-15-25-2 Lohmann 33-14-53-5 Sharpe 17-8-28-1 W.W. Read 3-0-9-0 Lockwood 15-9-12-1

SURREY

R. Abel	c Whitehead b Peel	5	c Wainwright b Peel		4
J. Shuter*	b Wainwright	24	b Peel		11
K.J. Key	c Lee b Peel	6	run out		33
W.W. Read	st Hunter b Peel	14	b Wainwright		4
G.A. Lohmann	st Hunter b Peel	6	b Wainwright		1
R. Henderson	b Whitehead	14	not out		59
W.H. Lockwood	st Hunter b Peel	13	b Wainwright		7
H. Wood+	c Wainwright b Whitehead	21	b Wainwright		8
J.W. Sharpe	b Whitehead	0	b Ulyett		14
J. Beaumont	c Hunter b Whitehead	2	not out		8
J.M. Read	not out	4			
Extras	(b3 lb2)	5	(b14 lb3)		17
TOTAL		114	(8 wkts)		166

FOW 1st: 11, 37, 43, 50, 59, 85, 85, 97, 105, 114
FOW 2nd: 17, 20, 25, 43, 77, 97, 105, 136

Bowling 1st: Peel 29-11-50-5 Wainwright 20-6-46-1 Whitehead 8.3-3-13-4

Bowling 2nd: Peel 42-16-51-2 Wainwright 36-15-43-4 Whitehead 14-6-27-0 Wade 15-8-13-0 Ulyett 9.3-4-15-1

SURREY WON BY TWO WICKETS

YORKSHIRE v. SOMERSET

Date: 19 July 1894   County Championship

Location: Huddersfield

The 1893 season had seen Yorkshire win its first official County Championship title and the team had begun the following campaign in a similarly successful vein. By the time Somerset had arrived at the Fartown ground their opponents had won seven of their first ten games, losing only to Surrey who themselves had won all of the first three Championships and were again in good form. A crowd of about 4,000 had turned up to watch Huddersfield's only county fixture of the season.

In complete contrast, Somerset came into this game having been humiliated by an innings at the hands of Lancashire at Old Trafford, the match taking only one day to complete. So dominant were their next opponents that their game with Yorkshire also lasted for only the first of its scheduled three days, the match lasting for just four hours and fifty minutes. The White Rose county's out-cricket was so efficient that Somerset lost all of their 20 wickets while scoring only 168 runs (each innings lasting 100 minutes) and *Wisden* described the home side's fielding as never having been surpassed. Brilliant catches were held and the game concluded with five minutes of the scheduled time remaining. Somerset remains the only team to lose two consecutive first-class matches each in a single day's play.

Although the conditions were not really adequate, the ground being very much in favour of the bowlers, this does not entirely excuse Somerset's lack of success. When play began at 12.05p.m. the pitch was

damp but played awkwardly rather than spitefully. Wickets fell in batches, especially so in their first innings, the first three falling for only nine runs – all to Ted Wainwright. Later, 40 for 3 became 41 for 6, and 71 for 6 became 74 all out. The main torturer was George Hirst who finished with five wickets for only nine runs in a 37-ball spell.

Yorkshire did not have matters all their own way when they batted and only three players passed double figures. Lord Hawke, who was, unusually for him, opening the batting, held the first part of the innings together in compiling what turned out to be his only half-century of the county season with neat and crisp strokes. He lost each of his first four partners to the slow left-arm spin of Edwin Tyler but found that Bobby Peel could help him in the resistance and the pair completed the only half-century stand of the entire game making 55 in thirty-five minutes. Thereafter, only Hirst, with some lusty hitting, made any real impact, putting on 38 for the eighth wicket with Bobby Peel, but Yorkshire had a lead of 99. There was a very uneven look to the scorecard as no one made a score of between 9 and 31, only three players making double figures.

Yorkshire captain Lord Hawke (pictured at the age of twenty-five) top scored in the Yorkshire innings as his side wrapped up a stunning first day victory.

YORKSHIRE v. SOMERSET

Once again it was Hirst and Wainwright who ensured that this would be enough as the West Country team collapsed for the second time. Hirst ended the game with match figures of 10 for 53 and Wainwright 8 for 85. They had bowled Yorkshire to a remarkable victory, which concluded at 6.20p.m. after the last three wickets had fallen for just two runs, by an innings and five runs. Thirty wickets had fallen for just 341 runs but the 'condition of the turf scarcely accounted' for such a downfall.

This result meant that Yorkshire and Surrey were now level at the top of the Championship table. It was the southern county that was the eventual winner, however, but by the narrowest of margins – one point. That Yorkshire finished seven points ahead of Middlesex shows how much of the title-chase had been a two-horse race.

YORKSHIRE v. SOMERSET

Somerset won the toss and elected to bat

Umpires: W. Clarke and J. Street

SOMERSET

Mr V.T. Hill	c Hunter b Hirst	25	b Hirst		9
Mr L.C.H. Palairet	c Hunter b Wainwright	1	c Jackson b Wainwright		7
Mr W.C. Hedley	c Moorhouse b Wainwright	0	c Jackson b Wainwright		18
Mr R.C.N. Palairet	c Hunter b Wainwright	1	b Hirst		0
Mr G. Fowler	c Hunter b Hirst	14	b Wainwright		14
G.B. Nichols	c Sellers b Wainwright	0	c Peel b Wainwright		5
Mr S.M.J. Woods*	c Mounsey b Jackson	19	c Wainwright b Hirst		9
Mr D.L. Evans	c Wainwright b Hirst	10	c Jackson b Hirst		2
Mr E.W. Ebdon+	c Tunnicliffe b Hirst	1	b Jackson		5
E.J. Tyler	b Hirst	0	c Moorhouse b Hirst		21
Rev A.P. Wickham	not out	2	not out		0
Extras	(b1)	1	(b4)		4
TOTAL		74			94

FOW 1st: 1, 1, 9, 40, 41, 41, 71, 71, 71, 74
FOW 2nd: 16, 22, 31, 45, 52, 68, 68, 92, 92, 94

Bowling 1st: Peel 9-2-18-0 Wainwright 13-3-42-4 Hirst 6.1-4-9-5 Jackson 2-0-4-1

Bowling 2nd: Hirst 17-4-44-5 Wainwirght 14-4-43-4 Jackson 2-0-3-1

YORKSHIRE

Lord Hawke*	b Woods	56
Mr F.S. Jackson	c&b Tyler	9
J. Tunnicliffe	c R. Palairet b Tyler	0
Mr A. Sellers	bTyler	1
J.T. Brown	c R. Palairet b Tyler	9
R. Peel	c Hill b Hedley	44
E. Wainwright	c Hill b Hedley	4
R. Moorhouse	c Tyler b Woods	2
J.T. Mounsey	b Woods	6
G.H. Hirst	not out	31
D. Hunter+	c Ebdon b Hedley	4
Extras	(b4 lb3)	7
TOTAL		173

FOW 1st: 12, 12, 26, 46, 101, 106, 111, 123, 161, 173

Bowling 1st: Tyler 21-4-68-4 Hedley 15.2-5-37-3 Woods 13-2-43-3 Nichols 8-2-18-0

YORKSHIRE WON BY AN INNINGS AND FIVE RUNS

WARWICKSHIRE v. YORKSHIRE

Date: 7, 8, 9 May 1896   County Championship
Location: Edgbaston

Lancashire had established the highest County Championship innings total (801) at Taunton against Somerset in the previous English season and so when the opportunity arose to knock the Red Rose county from the summit, Yorkshire captain Lord Hawke and his team seized their chance. Over 100 years on, the White Rose total of 887 remains a Championship record.

Warwickshire provided a 'fine wicket' for the fixture but, unfortunately for them, Lord Hawke won the toss and chose to bat first. Yorkshire opened their innings with F.S. Jackson and John Tunnicliffe and the pair compiled a first-wicket stand of 63 before Tunnicliffe was dismissed by Glover. Jackson, according to *Wisden*, 'played splendid cricket, while the Warwickshire bowling was at its best...' in making 117 (his highest score at Edgbaston and against Warwickshire). He was fourth out with the total at 211 and at that stage there must have been few thoughts of a record total. Bobby Moorhouse and all-rounder Ted Wainwright 'fairly collared the bowling'; thereafter, the latter became the second centurion of the innings before being run out for 126 made in two and a half hours at the crease. By the close of the first day, Yorkshire's total had reached 452 for 7 with Bobby Peel (37) and Lord Hawke (3) the overnight not-out batsmen. Despite the 'almost perfect condition' of the pitch, it seemed unlikely that Warwickshire would spend all of the second day in the field with only three Yorkshire wickets to claim. Hawke and Peel, with both their play and their tactics, ensured that was the case on day two. For the eighth wicket they added 292 runs, taking the score to 740. Hawke hit 21 boundaries, 'nearly all straight, hard drives' he later recorded, in his highest career score of 166. With the record now clearly in sight Yorkshire pushed on for the milestone and George Hirst (batting at no.10) looked set to be the fifth centurion of the innings as he 'hit freely' contributing 85 of the 136 runs added with Peel. Lancashire's record was reached and then passed by a further 86 runs as if to emphasise the point! The last Yorkshire wicket (David Hunter) brought final relief for the frazzled Warwickshire bowlers. Every member of the home side had bowled, except for Alfred Law, after two whole days in the field. Between them they sent down 274.3 five-ball overs and Henry Pallett had bowled 75.3 of those and finished with 4 for 184, a fine show of resilience. Peel finished unbeaten on 210, an innings that contained 16 fours and he batted for almost seven hours, although his scoring slowed considerably in the latter stages of his knock. Four centurions in the same innings was also the first instance of such a feat in first-class cricket.

The Yorkshire side beneath the Edgbaston scoreboard displaying their record-breaking innings total of 887. From left to right, back row: R.G. Barlow (umpire), G.H. Hirst, E. Wainwright, D. Denton, D. Hunter. Middle row: J. Tunnicliffe, F.S. Jackson, Lord Hawke (captain), F.W. Milligan. Front row: J.T. Brown, R. Peel, R. Moorhouse.

WARWICKSHIRE v. YORKSHIRE

Warwickshire finally began batting on the third and final morning of the match. The rules of the game at the time curiously precluded any declaration until the third day. Although dismissed for 203, Willie Quaife 92 not out in four hours, Warwickshire were never in danger of losing the game and only 11 wickets fell on the final day. Bainbridge was the only second-innings wicket to fall for the home side and he completed a no doubt unwanted double, having fielded throughout the previous highest recorded total in first-class cricket (843) made by the Australians against the Past and Present team of Oxford and Cambridge three years earlier. Lord Hawke and his side had clearly sacrificed any chance of victory in return for a record that, rightly or wrongly, ensured them a place in county cricket history.

WARWICKSHIRE v. YORKSHIRE

Yorkshire won the toss and elected to bat

Umpires: W.A.J. West and R.B. Barlow

YORKSHIRE

F.S. Jackson	c Law b Ward	117
J. Tunnicliffe	c Pallett b Glover	28
J.T. Brown	c Hill b Pallett	23
D. Denton	c W.G. Quaife b Santall	6
R. Moorhouse	b Ward	72
E. Wainwright	run out	126
R. Peel	not out	210
F.W. Milligan	b Pallett	34
Lord Hawke*	b Pallett	166
G.H. Hirst	c Glover b Santall	85
D. Hunter+	b Pallett	5
Extras	(b5 lb6 w4)	15
TOTAL		887

FOW 1st: 63, 124, 141, 211, 339, 405, 448, 740, 876, 887

Bowling 1st: Santall 65-9-223-2 Ward 62-11-175-2 Glover 30-1-154-1 Pallett 75.3-14-184-4 W.G. Quaife 8-1-33-0 Bainbridge 6-1-17-0 Hill 3-0-14-0 Lilley 6-1-13-0 W. Quaife 9-1-18-0 Diver 10-1-41-0

WARWICKSHIRE

H.W. Bainbridge*	c Hunter b Hirst	5	b Wainwright	29
W. Quaife	b Hirst	0	not out	18
W.G. Quaife	not out	92		
A. Law	c Jackson b Hirst	7		
A.F.A. Lilley+	b Hirst	0		
J.E. Hill	b Hirst	4		
E.J. Diver	b Peel	27		
H.J. Pallett	c Wainwright b Jackson	25		
S. Santall	b Hirst	29		
A.C.S Glover	b Hirst	1		
W. Ward	b Hirst	3		
Extras	(b4 lb3 w1 nb2)	10	(nb1)	1
TOTAL		203	(1 wkt)	48

FOW 1st: 0, 7, 25, 25, 31, 78, 117, 170, 176, 203
FOW 2nd: 48

Bowling 1st: Hirst 40.1-16-59-8 Peel 31-21-27-1 Jackson 18-9-23-1 Wainwright 16-7-35-0 Milligan 13-5-14-0 Brown 4-0-24-0 Moorhouse 4-1-11-0

Bowling 2nd: Peel 3-2-4-0 Wainwright 2.1-1-4-1 Milligan 5-1-15-0 Moorhouse 4-0-24-0

MATCH DRAWN

HAMPSHIRE v. YORKSHIRE

Date: 26, 27 May 1898

County Championship

Location: Southampton

Five hours and five minutes were all that it took for Yorkshire to inflict an innings defeat on Hampshire. The real loser in this contest was Harry Baldwin. He was the first Hampshire professional to be granted a benefit but must have wished that he had chosen a different game for his official benefit match. His own side went into the game somewhat depleted: four of their leading batsmen were Army officers and were all absent on military duties.

Before this game both teams had played just two Championship matches, with the home side drawing both of theirs while the visitors were also unbeaten but had gained a victory over Somerset. This was the game that saw the first-class debut of a certain Wilfred Rhodes and his remarkable match figures of 13 for 45.

Sadly, the whole of the play scheduled for the first day was lost owing to heavy rain. Despite this, Hampshire chose to bat on winning the toss. Their first innings began at noon and lasted a mere 30.4 overs. Schofield Haigh and Wilfred Rhodes (bowling for only the second time in a Championship match) bowled unchanged throughout, with the former being particularly unplayable (Haigh in fact was to record innings figures that were beaten by only two players in the whole season). Ten – for the first wicket – was the highest stand of the innings and the same total was to be the best individual score for the home side in the whole game. The previous day's downpour resulted in the ball rearing and moving unpredictably on a treacherous pitch. The surface was soft but had hardened enough on the top to make batting extremely problematical.

Yorkshire replied to Hampshire's 42 with 157 and this was a very good score in the conditions, particularly as the runs came at almost three per over. John Tunnicliffe batted throughout the visitors' innings, being last man out, and he received most support from Rhodes in that their partnership of 42 was the best of the match. Haigh, not to be kept out of the action, also reached double figures, as did George Hirst who, remarkably, did not bowl in either of Hampshire's innings.

The southern county's second innings was even shorter, lasting only 26.2 overs and finishing, as did the match, at 6.05p.m. There were a total of four ducks to add to the five from the first knock and Haigh's final match analysis was 14 wickets for 43 runs in 29 overs, 17 of which were maidens. Ten of his victims were clean bowled. Haigh is the least-known of the three great Yorkshire bowlers (Hirst and Rhodes being the others) who dominated this era. Although his main trade was to bowl right-arm fast-medium, he also had

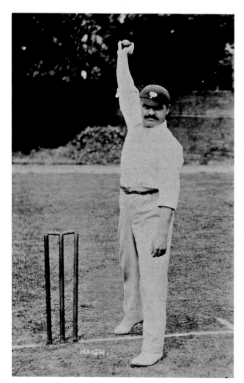

Schofield Haigh's 14 wickets – on a difficult Southampton pitch – included ten clean bowled.

the ability to bowl a sharply-turning off-break. Appearances in just 11 Test matches were scant reward for his skills.

In the return game at Huddersfield just two weeks later, Hampshire were again defeated by an innings. This time, however, the game lasted two days but the visitors' scores – 45 and 83 – meant that their batsmen had averaged a paltry 5.12 over the two games.

Yorkshire went on to win the Championship for the third time in the nine seasons since the competition had become official but Hampshire could finish only twelfth (out of a total of 14 teams). Rhodes' first campaign ended with him coming top of the national Championship bowling averages, taking 126 wickets at 13.84. This was indeed a significant start for someone who was to become a great player for both county and country.

HAMPSHIRE v. YORKSHIRE

Hampshire won the toss and elected to bat

Umpires: W.A.J. West and J. Lillywhite

HAMPSHIRE

Mr C.G. Ward	c Denton b Haigh	6	b Haigh	5
V.A. Barton	b Haigh	7	c Brown b Rhodes	3
Mr A.J.L. Hill	c Jackson b Rhodes	0	b Haigh	7
Mr W. Andrew	b Haigh	0	b Haigh	0
A.S. Webb	c Jackson b Rhodes	0	b Jackson	7
Mr B. Lamb	c Rhodes b Haigh	0	b Jackson	3
Mr C. Heseltine	b Haigh	6	not out	5
Mr D.A. Steele	c Jackson b Haigh	10	run out	0
Mr C. Robson*+	not out	6	b Haigh	0
H. Baldwin	b Haigh	6	b Haigh	0
E.E. Light	b Haigh	0	st Hunter b Haigh	4
Extras	(lb1)	1	(lb2)	2
TOTAL		42		36

FOW 1st: 10, 13, 13, 14, 14, 18, 23, 30, 36, 42
FOW 2nd: 8, 13, 15, 24, 27, 28, 28, 28, 28, 36

Bowling 1st: Haigh 15.4-10-21-8 Rhodes 15-8-20-2

Bowling 2nd: Haigh 13.2-7-22-6 Rhodes 7-3-10-1 Jackson 6-4-2-2

YORKSHIRE

J.T. Brown	b Baldwin	4
J. Tunnicliffe	b Baldwin	58
Mr F.S. Jackson	b Andrew	9
D. Denton	c Barton b Baldwin	3
E .Wainwright	st Robson b Light	8
G.H. Hirst	st Robson b Light	18
Mr F.W. Milligan	c Barton b Hill	2
W. Rhodes	c Andrew b Hill	28
Lord Hawke*	c Ward b Hill	0
S. Haigh	c Lamb b Baldwin	17
D. Hunter+	not out	4
Extras	(b4 lb2)	6
TOTAL		157

FOW 1st: 5, 18, 21, 41, 72, 79, 121, 125, 152, 157

Bowling 1st: Andrew 15-4-30-1 Baldwin 12.1-1-37-4 Light 11-0-44-2 Hill 18-5-44-3 Heseltine 2-0-6-0

YORKSHIRE WON BY AN INNINGS AND 79 RUNS

DERBYSHIRE v. YORKSHIRE

Date: 18, 19, 20 August 1898   County Championship

Location: Chesterfield

Queen's Park, Chesterfield had been opened in honour of Queen Victoria's Golden Jubilee in September 1887 and the scenic park cricket ground welcomed first-class cricket in late June 1898 (when a new cricket pavilion was opened) with a fixture against Surrey. Although Derbyshire were well beaten, the experiment was a financial success, so much so that county veteran Walter Sugg (who played once for Yorkshire in 1881) persuaded his committee to move his allocated benefit match, against Yorkshire, to the Chesterfield venue.

The previous season at Bramall Lane, J.T. Brown and 'Long John' Tunnicliffe – Yorkshire's opening batsmen – had established a new record first-wicket county stand of 378 against Sussex. At Chesterfield, they took their reputation to new heights, establishing a world record opening partnership in the first stand to exceed 500 in any first-class game. It would remain unsurpassed for thirty-four years before being beaten by two fellow Yorkshire opening batsmen. In front of a crowd of 6,000 Lord Hawke won the toss and, on a pitch described by the *Sheffield Telegraph* as a 'hard and perfectly true wicket...' and a 'wicket as hard as nails', the weak Derbyshire bowling was treated with 'scant respect'. The attack was depleted early on when George Davidson, who was not fully fit anyway, broke down after just one over. By the close of play on Thursday (day one) Yorkshire were 503 without loss; Brown on 270 and Tunnicliffe 214. White Rose captain Lord Hawke later recalled how he had wanted an innings that day and put himself at no.3 in the batting order: 'I actually kept my pads on from noon until tea-time, and then gave it up as a bad job.' The rules of the game at the time meant that no declaration was permissible until the last day and so Yorkshire batted on, under instruction from Hawke to 'hit out'. When the partnership had reached 554, made in 305 minutes (at a rate of 105 runs per hour), Tunnicliffe was dismissed for 243, his only double century and his highest first-class score. Five minutes later Brown 'knocked down his own wicket' having reached 300, his second triple century for the county following his 311 against Sussex the previous summer. He gave four chances during his five hours at the crease and both players struck 48 fours. Yorkshire were finally dismissed for 662 with Denton (45) the next highest scorer after Brown and Tunnicliffe.

Virtually the whole of the home side's bowling after the breakdown of George Davidson fell on the shoulders of his brother Frank and the thirty-eight-year-old G.G. Walker. Between them they bowled 94.3 of the 156.3 overs delivered. In all ten of the Derbyshire side bowled, William Chatterton was the one exception due to injury. Bad light ended day two early at 5.35p.m. Overnight rain made Derbyshire's

Extract from the match scorebook showing how Brown and Tunnicliffe compiled their record first-wicket stand.

DERBYSHIRE v. YORKSHIRE

task of trying to save the game virtually impossible. Yorkshire's seam attack, led by Jackson with four wickets, demolished Derbyshire's first innings batting for only 118. Forced to follow on 544 runs behind, the home side were 50 for 1 in their second innings by the end of the second day's play. Only Chatterton passed 50 in Derbyshire's second innings as Yorkshire registered their then largest innings victory margin, on route to their second Championship title under Lord Hawke. The one bright feature of the game from Derbyshire's point of view, and in particular for the match beneficiary Sugg, was that the proceeds amounted to £340!

DERBYSHIRE v. YORKSHIRE

Yorkshire won the toss and elected to bat

Umpires: H. Holmes and J.H. Holmes

YORKSHIRE

J.T. Brown	hit wkt b Storer	300
J. Tunnicliffe	c F. Davidson b Storer	243
Lord Hawke*	c Walker b Storer	14
D. Denton	b F. Davidson	45
G.H. Hirst	c G. Davidson b Walker	0
F.S. Jackson	c Storer b Walker	14
W. Rhodes	c Storer b Walker	6
F.W. Milligan	c Chatterton b F. Davidson	4
E. Smith	c Storer b Walker	4
S. Haigh	c Ashcroft b F. Davidson	13
D. Hunter+	not out	0
Extras	(b14 lb4 nb1)	19
TOTAL		662

FOW 1st: 554, 569, 578, 582, 600, 611, 625, 630, 662, 662

Bowling 1st: G. Davidson 1-0-3-0 Walker 55-11-199-4 F. Davidson 39.3-9-133-3 Sugg 5-0-27-0 Bagshaw 11-1-50-0 Storer 26-1-142-3 Ashcroft 6-1-21-0 Evershed 3-0-24-0 Wright 3-0-24-0 Charlesworth 7-1-31-0

DERBYSHIRE

S.H. Evershed*	c Hunter b Jackson	18	(1) b Smith	12
L.G. Wright	c Hawke b Hirst	0	(6) st Hunter b Rhodes	5
H. Bagshaw	c Haigh b Jackson	20	(5) b Jackson	2
W. Storer+	c Denton b Milligan	13	(2) c Rhodes b Jackson	25
W. Chatterton	b Milligan	6	(4) c&b Rhodes	54
G. A. Davidson	b Jackson	36	(7) lbw b Jackson	2
E. M. Ashcroft	c Hunter b Jackson	1	(9) not out	21
W. Sugg	c Brown b Smith	8	(-) b Rhodes	3
F. Davidson	c Haigh b Smith	3	(3) retired out	5
A. Charlesworth	c Haigh b Rhodes	7	absent hurt	0
G.G. Walker	not out	0	(10) b Haigh	7
Extras	(b5 lb1)	6	(b15 lb6)	21
TOTAL		118		157

FOW 1st: 4, 39, 48, 59, 76, 77, 102, 105, 118, 118
FOW 2nd: 20, 50, 74, 80, 95, 112, 118, 137, 157

Bowling 1st: Hirst 10-3-19-1 Jackson 28-12-52-4 Milligan 12-3-36-2 Smith 7.1-6-5-2 Rhodes 1-1-0-1

Bowling 2nd: Jackson 37-22-26-3 Milligan 4-2-6-0 Smith 21-10-35-1 Rhodes 29-13-47-3 Brown 4-1-9-0 Haigh 7.1-4-13-1

YORKSHIRE WON BY AN INNINGS AND 387 RUNS

YORKSHIRE v. WORCESTERSHIRE

Date: 7 May 1900   County Championship
Location: Bradford

For both teams this was the first first-class fixture of the season. Yorkshire had finished third in the Championship in 1899 while for Worcestershire it had been their first such campaign amongst the elite and they had finished twelfth (out of a total of 15 counties). The game between the two teams at Worcester had seen a narrow victory for the visitors whilst the return fixture had ended in a draw.

Anyone expecting an equal contest in this game, however, was to be cruelly denied. The visitors arrived in a state of some confusion: there had been late changes to the team as nearly all the amateurs were away and this left them 'deplorably weak in batting'. In addition, travel difficulties meant that only ten men had arrived by the time the toss took place. Even this had been delayed because of rain and play did not get under way until 12.20p.m. H.K. Foster, on winning the toss, decided to bat in conditions not conducive to doing so successfully as recent rain had 'considerably affected the ground', suggesting that he had not wanted to field with ten men.

Seventy minutes later, the side were all out and Stanley Gethin, who was one of three Worcestershire debutants, had still not arrived. Wilfred Rhodes and Schofield Haigh had bowled unchanged throughout the 25.3 overs rout and taken four wickets each. Only Ted Arnold, who was Worcestershire's one outstanding player from this era, put up much resistance and so well did he bat in the circumstances that he scored almost half of the eventual all out total of a miserable 43. The last seven wickets fell for only 24 runs.

Yorkshire's innings began just as badly and had soon progressed to a score of nine runs for four wickets – all of them to the right-arm pace bowling of George Wilson. What followed, however, was the highest partnership of the match as Ted Wainwright, with the highest score of the game, and George Hirst swung the match Yorkshire's way with solid batting in a stand of 47. Wainwright lasted until the score reached 75 for 6 when he was caught at the wicket. Haigh was the only other batsman to get into double figures and a further collapse of three wickets for four runs meant that the hosts were also all out for less than a hundred – although only just. Arthur Bannister, a debutant right-arm spin bowler, took five of the last six wickets to fall.

Although Worcestershire scored eight more runs in their second innings than they had in their first, they lasted ten minutes fewer and so the game was all over before six o'clock, Yorkshire

The Bradford Park Avenue pavilion, pictured around 1900, and the scene of Yorkshire's first day innings victory over Worcestershire that summer.

YORKSHIRE v. WORCESTERSHIRE

having no need to bat again. Rhodes and Haigh bowled unchanged again but the wickets were shared less equally this time round, the former being practically unplayable and making the batsmen feel 'almost helpless' in snaring seven victims and ending with match figures of 11 for 36 in only 24.1 overs.

The game contained 12 ducks (four for Yorkshire and eight for the visitors) and the match aggregate of 193 (for 29) is the fourth-lowest in Yorkshire's history. Furthermore, this game remains the only occasion in the history of the official County Championship in which a side has gained an innings victory in one day and scored fewer than 100 runs in doing so – a remarkable achievement. Worcestershire ended the season in twelfth place again and it may have eventually been some consolation to them that their opponents went on to win the title without losing a single game – the first team to do so.

YORKSHIRE v. WORCESTERSHIRE

Worcestershire won the toss and elected to bat

Umpires: W.A.J. West and R.G. Barlow

WORCESTERSHIRE

Mr H.K. Foster*	b Rhodes	6	b Haigh		6
Mr J. Howard	b Haigh	0	c Tunnicliffe b Rhodes		1
E.G. Arnold	c Hunter b Rhodes	20	b Rhodes		13
F.L. Bowley	b Haigh	5	st Hunter b Rhodes		12
J.B. Fereday	run out	0	c Hawke b Haigh		0
Mr A.W. Isaac	st Hunter b Rhodes	2	c Haigh b Rhodes		12
A. Bird	b Haigh	0	st Hunter b Rhodes		0
A.F. Bannister	b Rhodes	0	(9) not out		4
G.A. Wilson	c Washington b Haigh	1	(10) c Denton b Rhodes		0
T. Straw+	not out	2	(11) lbw b Rhodes		0
Mr S.J. Gethin	absent		(8) b Haigh		2
Extras	(b3 lb4)	7	(b1 lb1)		2
TOTAL		43			51

FOW 1st: 0, 18, 29, 32, 35, 40, 40, 43, 43
FOW 2nd: 4, 10, 27, 34, 34, 34, 47, 47, 47, 51

Bowling 1st: Rhodes 13-6-16-4 Haigh 12.3-3-20-4

Bowling 2nd: Rhodes 11.1-4-20-7 Haigh 11-0-29-3

YORKSHIRE

J.T. Brown, sen.	c Bowley b Wilson	2
J. Tunnicliffe	b Wilson	5
D. Denton	b Wilson	0
W.A.I. Washington	c sub b Wilson	0
E. Wainwright	c Straw b Bannister	34
G.H. Hirst	c Bird b Bannister	24
S. Haigh	b Bird	15
W. Rhodes	c&b Bannister	0
Lord Hawke*	c Foster b Bannister	0
J.T. Brown, jun	c Bird b Bannister	9
D. Hunter+	not out	6
Extras	(b1 lb3)	4
TOTAL		99

FOW 1st: 2, 3, 8, 9, 56, 75, 79, 79, 85, 99

Bowling 1st: Arnold 10-4-21-0 Wilson 15-7-25-4 Bannister 13.5-3-30-5 Bird 8-2-19-1

YORKSHIRE WON BY AN INNINGS AND FIVE RUNS

NOTTINGHAMSHIRE v. YORKSHIRE

Date: 20, 21 June 1901
Location: Trent Bridge

County Championship

Yorkshire came into this match in magnificent form. The county had won the 1900 Championship without losing a single game – the first team to do so – and had begun the 1901 campaign in a similarly imperious manner. They had won all of their first eight games, four being completed in two days, and by the time that they arrived at Trent Bridge their results totalled nine wins and two draws. Four of the victories had been by an innings and on seven occasions they had dismissed their opponents for fewer than 100 runs in an innings.

Having opted to bat first, Yorkshire soon lost Jack Brown but David Denton joined John Tunnicliffe and together they put on a stand of 62. This would turn out to be the highest of the innings as would Denton's eventual score of 73. Thereafter, wickets fell steadily on a pitch on which batting was never straightforward and Yorkshire were all out shortly before the end of the first day's play. John Gunn, with his left-arm medium pacers, induced a middle-order collapse in which four wickets fell for 19 and he finished with the best figures. There was just time for Nottinghamshire to score one run, off George Hirst, and lose one wicket, to Wilfred Rhodes, before stumps were drawn.

The following morning there was a delay of eighty minutes for rain and when play resumed Hirst, finding himself unable to get a foothold on the soft turf, was replaced. Schofield Haigh and Rhodes then took no longer than fifty-four minutes to dismiss the remaining nine batsmen on what was, by now, a very sticky wicket. The all out total of 13 was the lowest for the Championship and only nine scoring strokes (1 four, 1 two and 7 singles) were made from the 95 balls bowled.

Needless to say, the home side followed on and, with a much-changed batting order, produced a far better performance. Skipper Arthur Jones led the way and he and James Iremonger posted a partnership of 82 in an hour for the first wicket – the highest stand of the game. Sadly for Nottinghamshire, the dismissal of Jones was the prelude to another demise and all 10 wickets fell for the addition of only 91 runs. The first two batsmen and Gunn were the only ones to pass double figures with Charles Dench and Isaac Harrison both completing pairs. The latter played in the game only because of an act of generosity on Lord Hawke's part. After an hour on the first morning, Arthur Shrewsbury, regarded as the best wet-wicket batsman in the world, had split a hand when fielding at point and the Yorkshire captain allowed Harrison to replace him.

David Denton – top scorer in the match with an innings of 73 before Nottinghamshire were dismissed in just an hour.

NOTTINGHAMSHIRE v. YORKSHIRE

Hirst did most of the damage in Nottinghamshire's second innings and this meant that he, Rhodes and Haigh had taken 18 of their 20 wickets to fall in the match. Even though the home side had scored 160 more in their second innings than in the first, it was not enough to make the visitors bat again and the whole debacle was over in less than two days, the game concluding soon after six o'clock.

Six years later, Northamptonshire were dismissed for 12, by Gloucestershire, and these two scores remain the lowest for all County Championship games. Meanwhile, Yorkshire went on to retain the title by winning twenty of their twenty-seven fixtures, losing only one and, in the competition's percentage system, gaining 90.47% as against the 50% obtained by runners-up Middlesex. The win at Trent Bridge was the second in a run of seven consecutive victories, four being by an innings. Heady days indeed.

NOTTINGHAMSHIRE v. YORKSHIRE

Yorkshire won the toss and elected to bat

Umpires: G. Porter and W. Hearn

YORKSHIRE

J.T. Brown	c Anthony b Wass	6
J. Tunnicliffe	b Dixon	31
D. Denton	c W. Gunn b J. Gunn	73
Mr F. Mitchell	c&b J. Gunn	22
E. Wainwright	b J. Gunn	20
G.H. Hirst	c Harrison b J. Gunn	2
L. Whitehead	c W. Gunn b Hallam	27
Lord Hawke*	c&b Wass	1
S. Haigh	c Carlin b J. Gunn	5
W. Rhodes	c Wass b Hallam	11
D. Hunter+	not out	3
Extras	(b1 w1 nb1)	3
TOTAL		204

FOW 1st: 6, 68, 118, 148, 155, 158, 167, 190, 190, 204

Bowling 1st: Wass 26-3-84-2 Hallam 16.5-6-34-2 J. Gunn 33-15-49-5 Dixon 9-2-23-1 Jones 3-1-11-0

NOTTINGHAMSHIRE

A.W. Hallam	c Tunnicliffe b Rhodes	1	(10) b Hirst	0
C.E. Dench	c Wainwright b Haigh	0	(6) c Hunter b Hirst	0
W. Gunn	c Hunter b Rhodes	2	c&b Haigh	2
Mr A.O. Jones*	b Haigh	4	(1) c Mitchell b Wainwright	47
Mr J.A. Dixon	c Tunnicliffe b Rhodes	1	(4) b Rhodes	8
J. Carlin+	c Tunnicliffe b Rhodes	2	(7) b Wainwright	8
J.R. Gunn	c Hawke b Haigh	0	(5) c Hunter b Hirst	35
J. Iremonger	not out	0	(2) not out	55
I.M. Harrison	c Haigh b Rhodes	0	(8) b Hirst	0
G. Anthony	b Haigh	2	(9) b Hirst	5
T.G. Wass	st Hunter b Rhodes	1	b Hirst	0
Extras		0	(b13)	13
TOTAL		13		173

FOW 1st: 1, 3, 3, 4, 8, 8, 10, 10, 12, 13
FOW 2nd: 82, 90, 102, 155, 155, 164, 165, 173, 173, 173

Bowling 1st: Hirst 1-0-1-0 Rhodes 7.5-4-4-6 Haigh 7-2-8-4

Bowling 2nd: Hirst 12.1-2-26-6 Rhodes 22-4-53-1 Haigh 16-3-53-1 Wainwright 13-6-28-2

YORKSHIRE WON BY AN INNINGS AND 18 RUNS

YORKSHIRE v. SOMERSET

Date: 15, 16, 17 July 1901   County Championship
Location: Headingley

Yorkshire County Cricket Club, under the powerful leadership of Lord Hawke, was at its zenith during the first three seasons of the twentieth century. In 1900 they were all-dominant, unbeaten in 28 Championship fixtures with 16 outright victories and 12 drawn matches. Not since 23 August 1899 (versus Kent at Tonbridge) had they lost a county game by the time they gathered at Headingley in mid-July 1901 to take on Somerset. Undisputed Champions in 1900, they were to secure a hat-trick of titles, winning in 1901 and 1902. During those three golden years of success the Club played eighty Championship games and were beaten only twice – by Somerset on both occasions – the first triumph, at Headingley in the hot summer of 1901, was an epic confrontation.

The two sides had already fought out a close and thrilling contest at Taunton in May that year. Yorkshire had won a narrow one-wicket victory against the clock at Somerset to further extend their unbeaten run. Somerset travelled north on the back of a heavy ten-wicket defeat against Lancashire. Heavily reliant on amateurs (most were average club cricketers), Somerset were led by Australian-born Sammy Woods. Their most notable players included stylish amateur opening batsman Lionel Palairet, who played twice for England the following season, and all-rounder Len Braund. The West Country side was forced to call upon thirty-seven-year-old George Burrington from Tiverton, a godson of Sammy Woods, to help make up their final XI for the match at Leeds.

A hot and steamy opening day went the way of pre-match predictions and form. Woods won the toss for Somerset and gambled on batting first on a lively pitch. The decision was probably instantly regretted as both openers, Palairet and Braund, departed without scoring to George Hirst and Wilfred Rhodes respectively. Only Woods himself offered any real defiance with 46 in Somerset's paltry 87 all out, skittled

Yorkshire 1901 – unbeaten in a county game since 1899 before their clash with Somerset in July. From left to right, back row: E. Wainwright, L. Whitehead, W. Rhodes, D. Hunter. Middle row: G.H. Hirst, E. Smith, Lord Hawke (captain), F. Mitchell, J. Tunnicliffe. Front row: D. Denton, T.L. Taylor, J.T. Brown.

by Wilfred Rhodes' left-arm spin. Yorkshire's reply for a while faltered, 51 for 4 and then 86 for 6 against Cranfield and Gill. But Hirst's 61 and a partnership of 118 for the ninth wicket in only fifty-five minutes between Schofield Haigh, who smashed 96, and Rhodes (44) raised the home side to 325 all out at the end of the day's play – a lead of 238 and probably considered sufficient by the departing 10,000 spectators to ensure an innings victory. Certainly Somerset thought as much. That evening at a dinner party, Woods and his colleagues enjoyed the brandy provided by their host Mr Hepworth. He promised £100 to the county funds if Somerset won the game (the money was never paid). Woods himself placed long odds that Palairet would score a second innings hundred and provision was made to cancel their second night accommodation arrangements.

Much to their unexpected delight, the Somerset players were back at their hotel on the second evening. That was thanks in large part to the batting of Palairet, Braund and Francis Phillips. The openers atoned for their first-innings ducks by compiling a stand of 222 for the first wicket at a furious pace (they batted for two hours and twenty minutes). Yorkshire missed a run out chance and on 55 Braund was given not out when Tunnicliffe claimed a catch at slip. Umpire Mycroft's view had been impeded by the bowler and the decision was referred to Walter Wright, the square-leg umpire, who gave Braund the benefit of the doubt. Wright's verdict clearly ruffled the Yorkshire players; even the amiable Hirst was heard to say, whilst passing the umpire concerned later that day after Somerset's total had passed 500, 'Hey, Walter, tha knaws th'art a reight fooil.' Lord Hawke recognised the shift in fortunes: 'I never seemed to get my boys going again.' Palairet's elegant 173 took 220 minutes and included 28 fours. Braund went on to a stirring 107, made in 140 minutes with 15 fours. The third centurion of the Somerset second innings, Phillips, batted for 170 minutes and hit 13 fours and a five in his 122. Skipper Woods, who before play was still pessimistic enough about the day

Wilfred Rhodes had a fine match. With Haigh he added 118 for the ninth wicket in fifty-five minutes in his side's first innings and claimed 11 wickets in the game. His contribution was still not enough to prevent Somerset's extraordinary victory.

ahead to arrange an extra carriage to be coupled onto the late afternoon train, hit 66 batting with a runner having strained a leg. Somerset ended a breathtaking day on 549 for 5 (Hill [43] and Robson [10] the overnight not-out batsmen); Yorkshire were spent!

Somerset continued batting on the third morning on a now crumbling pitch. Woods called for the heavy roller, a decision Yorkshire's captain felt was 'unsporting', although Hawke would have applied a similar tactic had he been in Woods' position! Somerset's second innings closed on 630 made in 155 brutal overs of batting. Rhodes six second-innings wickets gave him 11 in the match whilst Hirst, complaining of sore feet, yielded 189 runs in his 37 overs of toil. Ted Wainwright also had more than a hundred runs against his bowling name.

Yorkshire's spirit was broken and they went in to bat needing a massive 393 to win. Any remaining thoughts that Yorkshire might yet salvage a draw were soon forgotten. Jack Brown went at 14, T.L. Taylor couldn't bat and although David Denton, Frank Mitchell and in particular John Tunnicliffe tried manfully to cope with the difficult batting conditions, Yorkshire slid from 104 for 4 to 113 all out. Beaumont Cranfield and Braund captured four wickets apiece to complete Somerset's bewildering 279-run victory. Woods and his heroes were roundly cheered by the crowd as they left the arena, and back in Somerset the game had been closely followed through telegraphed scores posted in shop windows. Lord Hawke was later to comment that the game 'was one of the best I ever lost...' Yorkshire's forty-eight-game unbeaten

YORKSHIRE v. SOMERSET

Headingley pictured around the time of Somerset's victory over Yorkshire in 1901.

The cartoonist 'Rip' captured the West Country's glory with his depiction of the Somerset captain Sammy Woods dealing with his county contemporary Lord Hawke.

run had been brought to an end. Somerset won only three other Championship matches that season from a programme of seventeen matches but they were back again the following season – this time at Sheffield – to inflict Yorkshire's only Championship defeat (by 34 runs) in 1902. The match at Leeds in 1901 was immortalised years later by Neville Cardus in his 1929 essay *West Country Lads* when he wrote: 'In one gaudy week in July 1901, piping hot history was made by these West Country gallants. At the time Yorkshire, as ever, were Champions. And they were invincible, Leeds, Sheffield and Bradford had watched Yorkshire man and boy for a summer and a half, and not once seen their darlings beaten.'

YORKSHIRE v. SOMERSET

Somerset won the toss and elected to bat

Umpires: W. Wright and T. Mycroft

SOMERSET

L.C.H. Palairet	b Hirst	0	c&b Brown	173
L.C. Braund	b Rhodes	0	b Haigh	107
A.G. Lewis	c Tunnicliffe b Rhodes	10	b Rhodes	12
F.A. Phillips	b Hirst	12	b Wainwright	122
S.M.J. Woods*	c Hunter b Haigh	46	c Tunnicliffe b Hirst	66
Mr V.T. Hill	run out	0	c Hirst b Rhodes	53
E. Robson	c Hunter b Rhodes	0	c Tunnicliffe b Rhodes	40
G.C. Gill	c Hunter b Rhodes	4	st Hunter b Rhodes	14
A.E. Newton+	b Haigh	0	c Taylor b Rhodes	4
G. Burrington	c Brown b Rhodes	11	st Hunter b Rhodes	15
B. Cranfield	not out	1	not out	5
Extras	(b2 lb1)	3	(b16 nb3)	19
TOTAL		87		630

FOW 1st: 0, 0, 16, 32, 38, 38, 64, 65, 86, 87
FOW 2nd: 222, 244, 341, 466, 522, 570, 597, 604, 609, 630

Bowling 1st: Hirst 12-5-36-2 Rhodes 16-8-39-5 Haigh 4-0-9-2

Bowling 2nd: Hirst 37-1-189-1 Rhodes 46.5-12-145-6 Haigh 20-4-78-1 Wainwright 34-3-107-1 Brown 18-1-92-1

YORKSHIRE

J.T. Brown	c Braund b Cranfield	24	c sub (L. Whitehead) b Gill	5
J. Tunnicliffe	c Newton b Gill	9	c Palairet b Braund	44
D. Denton	c Wood b Gill	12	b Braund	16
T.L. Taylor	b Cranfield	1	absent hurt	0
F. Mitchell	b Gill	4	(4) b Braund	21
G.H. Hirst	c Robson b Cranfield	61	(5) lbw b Braund	6
E. Wainwright	b Gill	9	(6) c Lewis b Cranfield	1
Lord Hawke*	b Robson	37	(7) c Burrington b Cranfield	4
S. Haigh	c Robson b Cranfield	96	(8) not out	2
W. Rhodes	c Lewis b Robson	44	(9) st Newton b Cranfield	0
D. Hunter+	not out	10	(10) c Woods b Cranfield	0
Extras	(b13 w5)	18	(b12 nb2)	14
TOTAL		325		113

FOW 1st: 13, 33, 44, 51, 55, 86, 142, 167, 285, 325
FOW 2nd: 14, 57, 91, 99, 104, 109, 109, 109, 113

Bowling 1st: Cranfield 27-5-113-4 Gill 23-2-105-4 Braund 5-0-33-0 Robson 10-1-35-2 Woods 5-1-21-0 Palairet 1-1-0-0

Bowling 2nd: Cranfield 18-5-35-4 Gill 4-1-23-1 Braund 15-3-41-4

SOMERSET WON BY 279 RUNS

YORKSHIRE v. AUSTRALIANS

Date: 2, 3 June 1902   First-class tour match
Location: Headingley

The very wet season of 1902 saw the Australians on English soil. One of the strongest touring parties of all time, Joe Darling's men won a thrilling Ashes series (2-1), recorded twenty-three victories in their thirty-nine tour matches and lost only to England (by one wicket) and Yorkshire in the first of two encounters that damp summer. As *Wisden* recorded in its review of the 1902 Australians, 'No travelling team ever strove harder for victory or more completely subordinated all personal considerations to the prime object of winning matches.'

Australia arrived at Headingley unbeaten on their tour hitherto but on the back of having been bowled out for only 36 in the first innings of the drawn Edgbaston Test by Yorkshire's George Hirst (3 for 15) and Wilfred Rhodes (7 for 17).

The opening day (Monday) of the Leeds match attracted a huge crowd (the turnstiles registered 33,705). Play started at 1.10p.m. following heavy rains during the weekend. Darling won the toss and chose to bat first on what was described as 'a very treacherous pitch'. By the end of his second tour to England, Victor Trumper would have forged a lasting reputation as one of the 'great' Australian batsmen. Despite the difficult batting conditions prevalent in 1902, Trumper amassed 2,570 runs including 11 centuries on the trip. Against Yorkshire, in four completed innings he made only 57 runs; 38 of his 'best' were made in Australia's first innings total of 131 (made in two-and-a-half hours) on day one at Headingley. Hirst and Stanley Jackson did most of the damage with four wickets apiece.

There was a thirty-five-minute delay before the home side's response as spectators spilled onto the outfield due to the numbers squeezed into the Leeds ground. The wet wicket continued to make batting very difficult and Yorkshire, 48 for 3 overnight, were forced to surrender a first-innings lead of 24. Lord Hawke decided to open the bowling with Hirst and Jackson in the Australian's second innings and the decision to hold back with Rhodes, even on such a soft, damp pitch, proved fully justified very quickly. Hirst, with his left-arm swerve, broke the back of the Australian batting, removing Trumper with 'the biggest

The Headingley crowd during Yorkshire's five-wicket victory.

swerve he ever sent down'. Six wickets were down by the time the Australians reached 20. Thereafter, Jackson, with his right-arm medium-fast bowling, applied the final humiliation. With the score on 23, Jackson removed the remaining four batsmen in one dramatic over. Syd Gregory took a single from the first ball, Bert Hopkins was trapped leg before wicket off the second, the third bowled James Kelly, Ernest Jones managed to keep out the fourth, before being comprehensively bowled off the fifth, and from the final delivery Bill Howell was caught behind by David Hunter to give Jackson four wickets in five balls. Australia had been dismissed for 23 in 84 deliveries in just over

YORKSHIRE v. AUSTRALIANS

seventy minutes! The target of 48 for a famous victory proved a difficult exercise for the Tykes against the bowling of Howell and Monty Noble. The temperament of young left-hander Irving Washington saw Yorkshire home by five wickets as he finished the match with an on-drive to the boundary to complete a wonderful triumph. As a lasting memento, the ball used to dismiss the Australian side for 23 was split into two and the inscribed halves presented to Jackson and Hirst. Yorkshire would have to wait another sixty-six years before the Australians were vanquished again.

YORKSHIRE v. AUSTRALIANS

Australians won the toss and elected to bat

Umpires: T. Mycroft and J. Moss

The damaged Kangaroo after Yorkshire's triumph over the Australians.

AUSTRALIANS

V.T. Trumper	c Denton b Jackson	38	b Hirst		7
R.A. Duff	b Hirst	12	c Jackson b Hirst		0
C. Hill	c Brown b Rhodes	7	st Hunter b Jackson		1
S.E. Gregory	c Jackson b Hirst	4	not out		10
J. Darling*	c Washington b Hirst	3	b Hirst		1
M.A. Noble	c Tunnicliffe b Jackson	0	b Hirst		2
W.W. Armstrong	c Denton b Jackson	3	b Hirst		0
A.J.Y. Hopkins	b Jackson	17	lbw b Jackson		0
J.J. Kelly+	b Hirst	23	b Jackson		0
E. Jones	c Haigh b Rhodes	20	b Jackson		0
W.P. Howell	not out	1	c Hunter b Jackson		0
Extras	(b1 lb1 w1)	3	(b2)		2
TOTAL		131			23

FOW 1st: 31, 42, 56, 64, 65, 65, 76, 102, 129, 131
FOW 2nd: 0, 7, 13, 14, 20, 20, 23, 23, 23, 23

Bowling 1st: Hirst 16.4-6-35-4 Rhodes 13-1-43-2 Jackson 13-2-30-4 Haigh 5-1-20-0

Bowling 2nd: Hirst 7-4-9-5 Jackson 7-1-12-5

YORKSHIRE

J.T. Brown	b Noble	13	c Howell b Noble		9
J. Tunnicliffe	c Armstrong b Howell	1	b Howell		3
D. Denton	c Hill b Noble	32	c Gregory b Noble		5
T.L. Taylor	b Noble	22	b Noble		11
F.S. Jackson	b Howell	0	c Kelly b Howell		6
G.H. Hirst	lbw b Howell	12	not out		0
W.A.I. Washington	b Howell	5	not out		9
S. Haigh	c Kelly b Noble	0			
Lord Hawke*	c Armstrong b Howell	3			
W. Rhodes	c Trumper b Howell	12			
D. Hunter+	not out	0			
Extras	(b7)	7	(b7)		7
TOTAL		107	(5 wkts)		50

FOW 1st: 5, 47, 48, 49, 69, 77, 80, 83, 107, 107
FOW 2nd: 19, 19, 25, 39, 41

Bowling 1st: Howell 20-4-53-6 Jones 3-0-17-0 Noble 16.3-6-30-4

Bowling 2nd: Howell 10-3-22-2 Noble 9.3-4-21-3

YORKSHIRE WON BY FIVE WICKETS

LEICESTERSHIRE v. YORKSHIRE

Date: 18, 19, 20 May 1905   County Championship
Location: Aylestone Road, Leicester

Yorkshire regained the Championship crown in 1905 having lost momentum following their hat-trick of titles between 1900 and 1902. The county's seventh County Championship-winning season since 1893 also witnessed another of George Hirst's colossal achievements in the Yorkshire record books. The Kirkheaton all-rounder, who had recorded a club record benefit amount (£3,703) in 1904, established the highest individual score by a Yorkshire player in first-class cricket, demoting J.T. Brown's innings of 311 against Sussex at Sheffield eight years earlier into second place.

The Aylestone Road ground was opened in 1901 and Leicestershire's match with Yorkshire there four years later was played on 'a shirt-front wicket'. Yorkshire arrived at Leicester on the back of some impressive early season form having won their first four Championship matches, three by an innings' margin. The home side. however. made a wonderful start to the game. Batting first after captain Charles de Trafford won the toss, Leicestershire compiled 419 with Cecil Wood carrying his bat through the innings to finish unbeaten on 160, made in six and a half hours and including 16 fours. He shared a fourth-wicket stand of 116 with Harry Whitehead (56) and a further 167 in a fifth-wicket partnership with left-hander Sam Coe who made exactly 100. Right-arm fast bowler William Ringrose and Wilfred Rhodes shared nine wickets. When Hirst went in to bat, Yorkshire had lost their first three batsmen ('Harry' Grimshaw, David Denton and John Tunnicliffe) with only 22 runs on the board. The further loss of Henry Wilkinson and Rhodes left the White Rose county struggling on 74 for 5. Schofield Haigh joined Hirst in a sixth-wicket stand of 144 to rescue the situation.

G. HIRST.
(YORKSHIRE.)

George Hirst – he registered Yorkshire's highest individual first-class score in this match having come to the crease when his side were 22 for 3.

Yorkshire ended the second day on 276 for 6, Hirst undefeated on 187. He and Hubert Myers extended their partnership to 183 and by the time Yorkshire's last wicket fell the total had reached 515. Hirst's record score of 341 occupied 415 minutes and included a six, 53 fours, 7 threes and 20 twos; he went in third wicket down and was last out. He gave only one real chance (a catch to short-leg when on 258), having survived a close shout for lbw (Hirst himself thought he was out!) before he had scored. Hirst's score would remain the highest individual innings made at the Aylestone Road ground. According to *Wisden*, he hit powerfully all round the wicket and gave his side a 96-run first-innings lead and a slim chance of pulling off an unlikely victory. Leicestershire crumbled to 72 for 7. With an hour left of play on the final day, and John

LEICESTERSHIRE v. YORKSHIRE

King and Albert Knight both carrying hand injuries, the match seemed destined to end with a Yorkshire win. But wicketkeeper David Hunter missed Arthur Davis and he and William Odell stayed together to save the match for Leicestershire.

Genuine concerns had been expressed about Hirst's fitness (due to leg troubles) at the start of the season but he dispelled all such fears. His performance with the bat at Leicester was typical of his batting form that summer – 1,972 runs for his county, over 2,000 in all first-class cricket, not to mention 100 wickets for Yorkshire with the ball. His 341 at Aylestone Road was one of five three-figure scores he made in 1905, which also included 232 not out against Surrey. His all-round form that season proved merely a prelude to the unimagined heights he reached in 1906.

LEICESTERSHIRE v. YORKSHIRE

Leicestershire won the toss and elected to bat

Umpires: J. Carlin and A. Millward

LEICESTERSHIRE

C.E. de Trafford*	c Grimshaw b Ringrose	58	c Wilkinson b Rhodes		11
C.J.B. Wood	not out	160	c Grimshaw b Ringrose		24
A.E. Knight	c Tunnicliffe b Rhodes	6			
V.F.S. Crawford	c Hunter b Ringrose	7	lbw b Rhodes		12
J.H. King	retired hurt	0			
H. Whitehead	c Hirst b Ringrose	56	(3) b Ringrose		12
S. Coe	c Hunter b Ringrose	100	(5) c Myers b Haigh		8
R.T. Crawford	c Myers b Ringrose	16	(6) b Rhodes		1
G.C. Gill	st Hunter b Rhodes	0	(8) b Haigh		1
A.E. Davis+	c Tunnicliffe b Rhodes	1	(7) not out		21
W.W. Odell	st Hunter b Rhodes	6	(9) not out		27
Extras	(lb6 w1 nb2)	9	(lb1 w2 nb1)		4
TOTAL		419	(7 wkts)		121

FOW 1st: 73, 81, 94, 210, 377, 405, 407, 409, 419
FOW 2nd: 19, 41, 56, 66, 70, 70, 72

Bowling 1st: Hirst 18-2-70-0 Myers 22-4-82-0 Ringrose 41-10-104-5 Rhodes 41.2-16-82-4 Haigh 12-0-43-0 Grimshaw 5-2-9-0 Denton 3-0-20-0

Bowling 2nd: Myers 6-0-34-0 Rhodes 23-13-22-3 Ringrose 15-0-53-2 Haigh 11-5-8-2

YORKSHIRE

H. Wilkinson	c Davis b Gill	14
C.H. Grimshaw	c Davis b Gill	2
D. Denton	lbw b R.T. Crawford	6
J. Tunnicliffe	c Whitehead b Gill	0
G.H. Hirst	c Whitehead b R.T. Crawford	341
W. Rhodes	c Davis b Gill	11
S. Haigh	c sub b Gill	31
H. Myers	c sub b Coe	57
Lord Hawke*	c&b R.T. Crawford	17
W. Ringrose	c Davis b Gill	8
D. Hunter+	not out	8
Extras	(b10 lb7 nb3)	20
TOTAL		515

FOW 1st: 3, 21, 22, 37, 74, 218, 401, 450, 483, 515

Bowling 1st: Gill 52-11-172-6 R.T. Crawford 47.5-18-117-3 Odell 26-7-61-0 Coe 28-5-100-1 Whitehead 12-1-29-0 W.F.S. Crawford 2-0-16-0

MATCH DRAWN

SOMERSET v. YORKSHIRE

Date: 27, 28, 29 August 1906   County Championship
Location: Bath

This was a match that was dominated by one man who secured a world record that has never been equalled. It occurred towards the end of a season during which the same player was producing another world record that has also never been equalled. The player concerned is George Herbert Hirst and the feat recorded in this match was that of scoring two centuries and twice taking five wickets in an innings.

This was Yorkshire's final Championship game of the season. Having won the title in the previous year, they again had been expected to challenge and did so but lost their penultimate match to Gloucestershire by only one run and this left Kent as champions for the first time.

Neither side was led by their regular captain, Lord Hawke being ill and Sammy Woods suffering from a leg injury. It was Ernest Smith who won the toss and Yorkshire began their innings well in very hot weather, so much so that they had scored 168 before lunch. Wilfred Rhodes and David Denton made 102 for the second wicket in only fifty-five minutes, before Hirst came in to make his first century of the game. His runs came from strokes all round the wicket, included 12 fours, and were scored out of a total of 157 made in 155 minutes while he was at the crease. Yorkshire ended the day on 347 for 8.

It took Somerset just twenty minutes to take the last two wickets at the start of the second day. Len Braund, who had started the innings bowling fast but later changed to leg-breaks, finished with six wickets. The home side then completely capitulated against the swing of Hirst, whose six wickets were the major contributory factor in Yorkshire gaining a big first-innings lead of 243. He concluded the innings by

GEORGE HIRST (YORKSHIRE).
"Always in the best of humours."

George Hirst – two centuries and 11 wickets in the fiery August heat at Bath.

taking the last two wickets in successive balls. Only Lionel Palairet put up much resistance; he scored 31 out of 41 'with all his old skill and grace'.

Smith decided not to enforce the follow on because of the extremely hot conditions. Yorkshire began their second innings at a tremendous rate and this was maintained throughout, the innings lasting only two hours. Hirst was promoted to no.3 and became only the second Yorkshire player to score two centuries in a match, emulating Denton who had done so earlier in the season. Hirst passed 2,000 runs for the third consecutive season, a 'fact greeted with considerable cheering', and shared an unbeaten double-century partnership with Rhodes, who also scored a century. Part of the innings descended into farce when Henry Marytn removed his wicketkeeping pads and gloves and went on to bowl. Palairet stood behind the stumps without such protection and, after the completion of an over, continued his own bowling spell from the same end.

An overnight declaration left Somerset with a mammoth target of 524 to win. Their batsmen again made very little impression, although their second innings, lasting 125 minutes, ended on a slightly higher score than their first effort. Hirst took five wickets, at a cheaper rate than in the first innings, and the visitors ran out as overwhelming victors. The last three wickets all fell to Schofield Haigh in one over.

Although two other players have also scored two centuries and taken ten wickets in a match, neither took five wickets in each innings so Hirst's feat remains unique in the entire history of first-class cricket. His aggregates at the end of an astonishing season were 2,385 runs and 208 wickets. No one has ever come near to equalling this amazing feat of endurance and concentration.

SOMERSET v. YORKSHIRE

Yorkshire won the toss and elected to bat

Umpires: W.A.J. West and A. Millward

YORKSHIRE

J. Tunnicliffe	c&b Braund	4	c Braund b Bailey	38
W. Rhodes	c Johnson b Bailey	64	not out	115
D. Denton	c Martyn b Braund	67		
Mr T.L. Taylor	c Poyntz b Mordaunt	41		
G.H. Hirst	c&b Mordaunt	111	(3) not out	117
H. Rudston	c Poyntz b Braund	21		
Mr E. Smith*	c Mordaunt b Braund	34		
S. Haigh	b Braund	1		
H. Myers	lbw b Braund	6		
D. Hunter+	b Mordaunt	8		
W. Ringrose	not out	2		
Extras	(lb7 w1 nb1)	9	(b2 lb6 w2)	10
TOTAL		368	(1 wkt dec)	280

FOW 1st: 24, 126, 161, 225, 308, 318, 323, 339, 356, 368
FOW 2nd: 78

Bowling 1st: Braund 38.3-3-125-6 Lewis 11-3-43-0 Bailey 19-2-83-1 Robson 14-2-37-0 Mordaunt 36-10-71-3

Bowling 2nd: Braund 6-0-44-0 Lewis 10-2-52-0 Bailey 10-2-36-1 Robson 4-0-39-0 Mordaunt 9-0-54-0 Phillips 2-0-19-0 Palairet 2-0-9-0 Martin 2-0-17-0

SOMERSET

Mr H. Martyn+	b Ringrose	2	c Rhodes b Hirst	23
Mr P.R. Johnson	b Rhodes	29	b Hirst	5
A.E. Lewis	b Hirst	3	b Hirst	0
L.C. Braund	b Hirst	28	b Ringrose	12
Mr L.C.H. Palairet*	b Hirst	31	c Hunter b Hirst	42
Mr F.A. Phillips	lbw b Rhodes	2	b Hirst	2
E. Robson	c Hunter b Hirst	3	b Haigh	26
Mr H.S. Poyntz	c Hirst b Rhodes	14	b Haigh	10
Mr F.M. Lee	not out	6	not out	6
Mr O.C. Mordaunt	b Hirst	3	lbw b Haigh	0
A.E. Bailey	b Hirst	0	b Haigh	2
Extras	(b3 lb1)	4	(b2 lb1 w1 nb2)	6
TOTAL		125		134

FOW: 1st: 7, 18, 62, 84, 87, 100, 103, 117, 125, 125
FOW 2nd: 9, 9, 28, 40, 87, 90, 121, 132, 132, 134

Bowling 1st: Hirst 26-3-70-6 Ringrose 12-5-21-1 Rhodes 14-4-28-3 Haigh 1-0-2-0

Bowling 2nd: Hirst 15-2-45-5 Ringrose 9-1-38-1 Rhodes 10-1-34-0 Haigh 5-1-11-4

YORKSHIRE WON BY 389 RUNS

SOMERSET v. YORKSHIRE

Date: 27, 28 August 1914   County Championship
Location: Weston-super-Mare

War against Germany had been declared for almost a month by the time Yorkshire arrived at the Clarence Park ground in late August for the first-ever Weston County Cricket Week. Yet, despite the fearful backdrop against which this fixture was played, the locals were there in number on the Festival's opening day (gate receipts amounted to £40 and the crowd was estimated at 'nearly 2,000'). Somerset, without the services of Jack White, Peter Johnson and the Rippon brothers (Arthur and Albert), fielded one of their weakest sides that summer whilst an all professional Yorkshire XI was led by George Hirst. The Yorkshire bowling partnership of Major Booth (right-arm fast-medium) and Alonzo Drake (slow left-arm) had crushed Gloucestershire at Bristol inside two days prior to the Weston game.

A poorly prepared and newly laid pitch greeted the two sides and, having won the toss, Yorkshire batted first. Such was the state of the pitch that from early on pieces of still-damp turf were cut out by the ball. The visitors attacked the Somerset bowling in the first hour of play but wickets tumbled in the process. The first fifty minutes yielded 80 runs, although Yorkshire lost half of their wickets. David Denton's 52 (7 fours) and 51 from the all-rounder Drake raised Yorkshire's first innings total to 162, made in only two and a half hours batting. Yorkshire's relatively low total was brought into some kind of perspective when the home side batted. In just one hour, Somerset were dismissed for a paltry 44. Booth and Drake, who made the ball 'turn quickly and queerly', took five wickets each. Ernest Robson was the only batsman to reach double figures. He made 19 of the 22 runs scored while he was at the wicket. The only 'stand' of any note was 12 added by the ninth-wicket pair. Carrying forward a priceless and significantly large first innings lead of 118, Yorkshire finished an eventful opening day on 59 for 4 when they batted for a second time. Twenty-four wickets had fallen in the day.

Wilfred Rhodes top scored with 25 as Yorkshire were dismissed for 112 on a bright, sunny second morning. That left Somerset a victory target of 231 – a most unlikely proposition considering the state of the pitch and Yorkshire's in-form bowlers. The Somerset wickets began to tumble soon after the lunch break. The continued decline in the pitch was graphically illustrated when Len Braund was hit on the cheek by the first ball he received. The first eight Somerset wickets fell for 52 runs and all eight were captured by Drake with his unplayable slow left-arm stuff. The possibility had dawned that the Rotherham-born all-rounder might become the first Yorkshire bowler to claim all ten wickets in a first-class innings. Major Booth, who had again bowled as Drake's

YORKSHIRE V. SOMERSET.

BRILLIANT PERFORMANCE BY DRAKE.

ALL TEN WICKETS IN AN INNINGS.

(From our Cricket Representative.)

Weston-super-Mare, Friday.

The *Yorkshire Post* headlines from August 1914 declaring Drake's bowling feat at Weston-super-Mare.

38

only partner, now clearly offered only token company, so provided Drake with every opportunity to achieve the historic feat. Despite resistance from Philip Hope and John Harcombe, Drake was not to be denied. At 3.30p.m. on the second day Yorkshire were victors by 140 runs (their eleventh victory in twelve matches) and Drake had reached the pinnacle of his meteoric career. His 10 wickets were taken in the space of only 42 deliveries and his match figures were 15 for 51 in just 15.5 overs.

Tragically, by the time first-class cricket resumed after the War in 1919, both Drake (heart condition) and Booth (killed in action) were in their graves and Yorkshire had lost two of their most promising cricketers.

SOMERSET v. YORKSHIRE

Yorkshire won the toss and elected to bat

Umpires: A.E. Street and A. Millward

YORKSHIRE

M.W. Booth	c Poyntz b Bridges	1	b Bridges		9
B.B. Wilson	c Saunders b Bridges	20	b Bridges		9
D. Denton	c Chidgey b Hylton-Stewart	52	c Saunders b Bridges		0
R. Kilner	b Hylton-Stewart b Bridges	2	c Braund b Bridges		4
W. Rhodes	c&b Hylton-Stewart	1	lbw b Robson		25
T.J. Birtles	lbw b Braund	16	b Robson		10
A. Drake	c Harcombe b Braund	51	c Hope b Robson		12
P. Holmes	b Bridges	7	not out		3
G.H. Hirst*	c Bisgood b Bridges	5	c Saunders b Robson		10
E. Oldroyd	not out	0	b Hylton-Stewart		23
A. Dolphin+	b Braund	0	b Robson		0
Extras	(b5 nb2)	7	(b4 lb2 w1)		7
TOTAL		162			112

FOW 1st: 4, 45, 54, 59, 80, 114, 132, 162, 162, 162
FOW 2nd: 9, 9, 32, 53, 69, 85, 85, 108, 112, 112

Bowling 1st: Robson 14-5-45-0 Bridges 17-1-59-5 Hylton-Stewart 9-0-38-2 Braund 8.4-2-13-3

Bowling 2nd: Robson 14-2-38-5 Bridges 14-1-54-4 Hylton-Stewart 2-0-6-1 Braund 4-2-7-0

SOMERSET

B.L. Bisgood	c&b Booth	6	c Dolphin b Drake		11
L.C. Braund	b Drake	1	b Drake		9
E. Robson	c Rhodes b Booth	19	c Birtles b Drake		3
B.D. Hylton-Stewart	b Drake	1	st Dolphin b Drake		3
W. Hyman	b Drake	1	st Dolphin b Drake		4
E.S.M. Poyntz*	b Drake	0	c Oldroyd b Drake		5
P.P. Hope	b Booth	3	c&b Drake		19
H.W. Saunders	b Drake	0	b Drake		0
H.D. Harcombe	not out	5	b Drake		26
J.F. Bridges	c Drake b Booth	7	not out		1
H. Chidgey+	c Holmes b Booth	0	b Drake		4
Extras	(b1)	1	(b4 nb1)		5
TOTAL		44			90

FOW 1st: 6, 14, 24, 28, 28, 28, 32, 32, 44, 44
FOW 2nd: 13, 20, 25, 28, 33, 38, 49, 52, 89, 90

Bowling 1st: Booth 8-0-27-5 Drake 7-1-16-5

Bowling 2nd: Booth 9-0-50-0 Drake 8.5-0-35-10

YORKSHIRE WON BY 140 RUNS

YORKSHIRE v. NORTHAMPTONSHIRE

Date: 27, 28 July 1921   County Championship

Location: Harrogate

This was the match that produced the most emphatic victory in Yorkshire's entire history and, given their lowly status, it is not surprising to find that their opponents were Northamptonshire. The Midland county had become the sixteenth team to enter the County Championship in 1905 and for nine of their first twelve seasons they finished in the bottom half of the table.

Yorkshire, meanwhile, were the leading county, having already won the title on ten occasions – three more than Surrey, their closest rivals. They had not been out of the top four for each of the last five seasons and, before this encounter, had won all of their six previous games. Four of these victories were by an innings and included a game at Northampton just three weeks previously in which the visitors had lost only six wickets and the home side had been bundled out for 81 and 108, the margin being an innings and 194 runs. The game had finished shortly after four o'clock on the second day.

The parallels between that game and this one are there for all to see. The major differences are that Yorkshire lost only four wickets in scoring 165 more runs, that Northamptonshire scored 38 runs fewer and that the game was forty minutes shorter.

Northamptonshire's early dismissal of Herbert Sutcliffe was their best moment in this match but merely acted as a prelude to a 160-run stand for the second wicket between Percy Holmes and Edgar Oldroyd. The former was at his fleet-footed best while Oldroyd contributed a display of sound technique and solid-ity. Geoffrey Wilson also lent support for a while but then Roy Kilner joined Holmes and the result was a partnership of 299 that still stands as the county's second-best for the fourth wicket. Holmes, who gave two chances but only after passing 200, hit one six and 46 fours, with Kilner hitting 26 fours.

Percy Holmes – an unbeaten double hundred in Yorkshire's largest-ever innings victory.

Northamptonshire's ten bowlers were all treated with the same scant regard, the runs being scored at a rate of just under four and a half per over, full advantage being taken of the short boundaries. Of the main bowlers, only the right-arm fast-medium of Albert Thomas conceded fewer than three runs per over. Kilner had scored 166 in the previous encounter between these two teams; his seven first-class innings in between showed a highest score of 39!

The second day produced considerable contrast when compared with the first; there were 16 more wickets, 397 fewer runs, eight fewer bowlers and two and a half hours' less play. An overnight declaration left the visitors needing 399 to make Yorkshire bat again but they came nowhere near doing so. Emmott Robinson bowled 27 overs and achieved match figures of 10 for 70; Abe Waddington's 26 overs

YORKSHIRE v. NORTHAMPTONSHIRE

produced 9 for 61 as the two fast-medium pacemen – the former right-arm and the latter left-arm – demolished the 'deplorable' Northamptonshire batting, only one player showing 'any approach to county' standard.

The two innings produced eight 'ducks', a highest score of 35 and a highest partnership of 25. Only Fred Walden was able to hold up the procession of batsmen and only he made a combined total of runs that was higher than that of the extras!

Following this match, during which Holmes was on the field for the whole game, Yorkshire's campaign lost its way somewhat. They won only three of their last eight matches and finished only in third place. Northamptonshire, meanwhile, finished thirteenth and two years later ended up in last place. Although it was the first time they had done this, it was the start of an unenviable record – ten 'wooden spoons', more than any other county.

YORKSHIRE v. NORTHAMPTONSHIRE

Yorkshire won the toss and elected to bat

Umpires: J. Moss and W. Reeves

YORKSHIRE

P. Holmes	not out	277
H. Sutcliffe	lbw b Murdin	3
E. Oldroyd	run out	71
G. Wilson*	b Thomas	31
R. Kilner	b Woolley	150
W. Rhodes	not out	6
E. Robinson		
D.C.F. Burton		
G.G. Macaulay		
A. Waddington		
W.R. Allen+		
Extras	(b1 lb5 w3 nb1)	10
TOTAL	(4 wkts dec)	548

FOW 1st: 15, 175, 231, 530

Bowling 1st: Murdin 40-4-147-1 Woolley 23-2-90-1 Thomas 25-7-66-1 Wells 3-0-10-0 Walden 10-0-73-0 Thompson 8-0-50-0 Haywood 4-1-23-0 Timms 3-0-36-0 Adams 4-0-23-0 Bellamy 2-0-20-0

NORTHAMPTONSHIRE

C.N. Woolley	b Waddington	10	c Holmes b Robinson	5
R.A. Haywood	c Sutcliffe b Robinson	9	c&b Waddington	0
F.I. Walden	b Waddington	9	c Holmes b Robinson	35
W.W. Timms	lbw b Robinson	0	b Robinson	0
G.J. Thompson	b Waddington	2	c Allen b Waddington	0
W. Wells	c Holmes b Robinson	14	c Oldroyd b Robinson	5
J.V. Murdin	c Allen b Waddington	0	lbw b Robinson	8
W. Adams*	b Waddington	4	run out	0
B.W. Bellamy	b Robinson	0	c Allen b Robinson	16
W.A. Buswell+	not out	0	not out	2
A.E. Thomas	b Waddington	0	b Waddington	12
Extras	(b4 lb4 nb2)	10	(b5 nb5)	10
TOTAL		58		93

FOW 1st: 19, 27, 32, 38, 38, 39, 55, 57, 57, 58
FOW 2nd: 0, 11, 11, 24, 29, 54, 54, 70, 80, 93

Bowling 1st: Robinson 11-3-27-4 Waddington 10.5-3-21-6

Bowling 2nd: Robinson 16-7-43-6 Waddington 15.1-3-40-3

YORKSHIRE WON BY AN INNINGS AND 397 RUNS

GLOUCESTERSHIRE v. YORKSHIRE

Date: 9, 10, 11 August 1922   County Championship
Location: Bristol

Yorkshire came to Bristol carrying an unbeaten run that stretched back to 19 June and were strong contenders for the Championship. Gloucestershire, meanwhile, were languishing in the lower half of the table and were not expected to provide much of a threat. Charlie Parker, however, was playing in his benefit match and had other ideas.

The first day's play could not start until 3.00p.m. and there was also a break for bad light later in the afternoon. The upshot of these truncated sessions was that the home side had progressed to only 92 for 4 by the close of play. The pitch was a difficult one for batting and only a further 80 runs were scored on the second day before the remaining six wickets had fallen. The two spinners, Roy Kilner and Rockley Wilson – who was captain for this game – had such a stranglehold on the proceedings that only 42 runs were scored from their combined total of 45 overs.

On such a pitch, Parker was also in his element; although his bowling was of the slow left-arm variety he opened the attack with Percy Mills and the two bowled throughout the brief innings, with the former returning nine for 36 – the fourth best analysis for the entire Championship season. The whole innings was over in just seventy minutes and Gloucestershire were batting again at 4.00p.m., having needed only 20.2 overs to dismiss the northern county. Only four batsmen passed double figures – there were

Edgar Oldroyd – a vital half century and fifth-wicket partnership with Emmott Robinson in Yorkshire's second-innings run chase.

four 'ducks' – and the highest partnership was the 26 put on for the third wicket by Herbert Sutcliffe and Kilner who top-scored with 14.

In the prevailing conditions, a first-innings lead of 106 ought to have been a match-winning one but Wilfred Rhodes had other ideas. He had seen what a bowler of his type could do with the new ball and decided that he should copy the tactic. The result was that he took five of the first seven wickets to fall and the home side struggled so much that their all out total of 58 was eked out over a period of two hours and took 39.1 overs. Wilson again proved virtually unplayable and was struck for only seven runs in his 11.1 overs. The home side did not help themselves by engineering two run-outs and only Alfred Dipper, with 16, reached double figures.

Yorkshire began their quest for the victory target of 165 just before the end of play and had reached 8 for 0 by the close. This meant that at least a part of all four innings had been seen on this remarkable middle day's play that had produced only 212 runs but 26 wickets.

Parker and Mills were again entrusted with most of the work as the final day began and, with two vic-

GLOUCESTERSHIRE v. YORKSHIRE

tims each and Yorkshire on 71 for 4, looked to be taking Gloucestershire to victory. The visitors' response was then to produce the best batting of the match and Edgar Oldroyd and Emmott Robinson saw that not another wicket was lost. They rode their luck – they needed to – but a partnership of 96, easily the highest of the match, saw them home. The winning run was hit at 3.20p.m. and a match with an amazing turn-around had ended (for the victors) eventually in relative comfort.

Yorkshire lost only one of their remaining six matches and carried off the title for the first of four consecutive seasons – the first time that this had been achieved. But the 1922 Championship would not have been theirs without a miraculous change of fortunes at Bristol.

GLOUCESTERSHIRE v. YORKSHIRE

Gloucestershire won the toss and elected to bat

Umpires: W. Phillips and W.A.J. West

GLOUCESTERSHIRE

C.L. Townsend	b Waddington	19	b Rhodes	3
A.E. Dipper	c Waddington b R. Kilner	54	b Rhodes	16
H. Smith+	c Dolphin b Macaulay	4	lbw b Rhodes	7
B.H. Lyon	c Oldroyd b Waddington	2	lbw b Waddington	0
Capt M.A. Green	b R. Kilner	15	run out	9
P.F.C. Williams*	b R. Kilner	19	st Dolphin b Rhodes	7
F.G. Robinson	c Oldroyd b Wilson	8	b Rhodes	4
P.T. Mills	b Rhodes	17	c Robinson b Wilson	2
C.W.L. Parker	c Rhodes b Macaulay	7	not out	2
E.G. Dennett	c Rhodes b Macaulay	7	run out	1
J. Bessant	not out	9	c Macaulay b Wilson	1
Extras	(b4 lb4 nb3)	11	(b2 lb3 nb1)	6
TOTAL		172		58

FOW 1st: 31, 38, 45, 80, 114, 129, 129, 152, 156, 172
FOW 2nd: 12, 21, 22, 32, 41, 45, 52, 52, 57, 58

Bowling 1st: Waddington 21-6-39-2 Robinson 7-3-17-0 Macaulay 25-7-48-3 R. Kilner 27-14-26-3 Wilson 18-9-16-1 Rhodes 8-4-15-1

Bowling 2nd: Rhodes 20-11-24-5 R. Kilner 3-0-13-0 Waddington 5-2-8-1 Wilson 11.1-7-7-2

YORKSHIRE

P. Holmes	c Smith b Parker	0	b Mills	6
H. Sutcliffe	lbw b Parker	11	b Mills	17
E. Oldroyd	lbw b Parker	0	not out	63
R. Kilner	b Parker	14	b Parker	0
W. Rhodes	lbw b Mills	12	c Bessant b Parker	22
E. Robinson	b Parker	1	not out	39
N. Kilner	b Parker	5		
G.G. Macaulay	b Parker	8		
A. Dolphin+	b Parker	0		
A. Waddington	b Parker	0		
E.R. Wilson*	not out	13		
Extras	(b1 nb1)	2	(b12 lb8)	20
TOTAL		66	(4 wkts)	167

FOW 1st: 0, 0, 26, 27, 39, 44, 45, 45, 45, 66
FOW 2nd: 19, 44, 45, 71

Bowling 1st: Parker 10.2-2-36-9 Mills 10-2-28-1

Bowling 2nd: Parker 35-17-46-2 Mills 38-19-45-2 Dennett 11-3-30-0 Bessant 7-3-26-0

YORKSHIRE WON BY SIX WICKETS

YORKSHIRE v. SUSSEX

Date: 15, 17, 18 August 1925   County Championship
Location: Bradford Park Avenue

Forty-six-year-old Major Arthur Lupton led Yorkshire to their fourth successive Championship title in 1925 following a hat-trick of crowns under Geoffrey Wilson. Lupton, whose only previous first-class appearance before 1925 had been seventeen years earlier in 1908, brought a needful level of discipline to both the job and the side. Although well past his best in terms of playing ability, he was ever-present in the Yorkshire ranks that summer. Lupton's team became the first county side to win four successive Championships since the official competition had begun in 1890. Moreover, they achieved the landmark in grand style by remaining unbeaten in their 32 matches (won 21, drawn 11) – the first time this had been done since 1908 (Yorkshire that year also). The closest they came to defeat was in a dramatic encounter at Bradford, in their last home match of the season against Sussex.

It was the beginning of Bowling Tide, the local industrial holiday, and large numbers of locals had therefore already left the city when the match got underway. Even so, there was a good crowd (12,000 for the match paid £8,153) over the three days.

The Sussex bowling trio of Maurice Tate, Albert Wensley and Reverend Francis Browne managed to limit Yorkshire's first-innings total to only 119 on a damp pitch. Edgar Oldroyd and Abe Waddington were joint top scorers with 19, the latter unbeaten. The popular Wombwell all-rounder Roy Kilner (he had enjoyed a record-breaking county benefit match against Middlesex earlier in the season – £4,106) strangled the Sussex response with figures of 5 for 14 from 15.2 overs of slow left-arm bowling. Only the amateur Richard Young (26) made a meaningful contribution and the visitors conceded a first-innings lead of 32.

Building on their advantage, Yorkshire performed far better with the bat second time around. Herbert Sutcliffe, George Macaulay and Emmott Robinson all made useful runs, whilst Oldroyd, in making the top score of 77, 'maintained an impregnable defence for three hours and fifty minutes,' recorded *Wisden*. Browne's impressive bowling brought him 7 for 62 and 10 wickets in the match. Sussex required 263 for a famous upset and to register Yorkshire's first defeat of the summer. The openers Ted Bowley and Tate made a fine start in pursuit of their target with a first-wicket stand of 79 before Tate was bowled by

Above left: George Macaulay 'pulled the game out of the fire...' according to *Wisden* with his second-innings bowling.

Above right: The Yorkshire side of 1925. From left to right, top row: A. Waddington, E. Robinson, P. Holmes. Second row: H. Sutcliffe, Major A.W. Lupton (captain), R. Kilner. Third row: G.G. Macaulay, W. Rhodes, A. Dolphin. Fourth row: M. Leyland, E. Oldroyd.

YORKSHIRE v. SUSSEX

Kilner for 39. Young made only 11 but Tommy Cook helped Bowley to take the score to 186. By lunch on the final day, Sussex, with six wickets in hand, needed only 40 more runs to win.

Legend has it that Yorkshire bowler George Macaulay drank champagne during the interval and, whilst this will remain folklore, what is certain is that Macaulay utterly transformed the complexion of the match in what must have been a stirring afternoon session. In 5.3 overs he took five wickets for eight runs. In each of his first three overs after lunch he captured a wicket. Exhausted from his efforts, Macaulay's final innings figures read: 22.3 overs, seven wickets for 67 runs, including the vital wicket of Bowley who had batted over four hours in making 105. Poor Sussex must have left Bradford, bound for their next match against Leicestershire, totally shell-shocked and bewildered by the deeds of Macaulay earlier that afternoon.

YORKSHIRE v. SUSSEX

Yorkshire won the toss and elected to bat

Umpires: W. Reeves and J. Stone

YORKSHIRE

Batsman	Dismissal 1st	1st	Dismissal 2nd	2nd
P. Holmes	b Wensley	10	c Cox b Wensley	7
H. Sutcliffe	c Wensley b Tate	9	c Cox b Browne	38
E. Oldroyd	c Cook b Wensley	19	c Wensley b Cox	77
M. Leyland	lbw b Browne	18	c Bowley b Browne	1
W. Rhodes	c Bowley b Wensley	15	b Browne	3
R. Kilner	c Bowley b Cox	3	c Bowley b Browne	0
E. Robinson	b Browne	17	c Gilligan b Bowley	54
G.G. Macaulay	c Cornford b Tate	0	c Parks b Browne	39
A. Waddington	not out	19	b Browne	2
Major A.W. Lupton*	c Cox b Browne	0	not out	0
A. Dolphin+	b Wensley	0	b Browne	0
Extras	(b2 lb5 nb2)	9	(b6 lb2 w1)	9
TOTAL		119		230

FOW 1st: 17, 29, 38, 72, 75, 82, 85, 110, 110, 119
FOW 2nd: 17, 69, 73, 77, 77, 179, 228, 228, 230, 230

Bowling 1st: Tate 24-8-36-2 Wensley 20.1-6-44-4 Cox 11-6-13-1 Browne 8-3-17-3

Bowling 2nd: Tate 23-6-55-0 Wensley 22-3-52-1 Browne 27.5-4-62-7 Cox 17-9-25-1 Bowley 5-2-17-1 Parks 2-0-10-0

SUSSEX

Batsman	Dismissal 1st	1st	Dismissal 2nd	2nd
E.H. Bowley	lbw b Robinson	8	c Dolphin b Macaulay	105
M.W. Tate	c Dolphin b Robinson	9	b Kilner	39
R.A. Young	c Holmes b Robinson	26	c Oldroyd b Macaulay	11
T.E.R. Cook	run out	1	b Waddington	42
G. Cox	lbw b Kilner	4	b Macaulay	16
R.L. Holdsworth	c Oldroyd b Kilner	11	b Macaulay	2
J.H. Parks	c Holmes b Kilner	7	b Macaulay	3
A.E.R. Gilligan*	c Waddington b Kilner	7	c Robinson b Macaulay	3
A.F. Wensley	lbw b Macaulay	6	lbw b Kilner	2
W. Cornford+	not out	1	c Waddington b Macaulay	0
F.B.R. Browne	b Kilner	0	not out	0
Extras	(b6 nb1)	7	(b8 lb4 nb4)	16
TOTAL		87		239

FOW 1st: 9, 20, 30, 37, 55, 64, 71, 85, 87, 87
FOW 2nd: 79, 105, 186, 223, 225, 228, 229, 235, 239, 239

Bowling 1st: Robinson 18-5-38-3 Macaulay 12-7-21-1 Kilner 15.2-9-14-5 Waddington 3-1-7-0

Bowling 2nd: Robinson 22-9-59-0 Macaulay 22.3-1-67-7 Waddington 15-3-42-1 Kilner 32-13-35-2 Rhodes 11-3-20-0

YORKSHIRE WON BY 23 RUNS

YORKSHIRE v. WARWICKSHIRE

Date: 16, 18 May 1931   County Championship
Location: Headingley

Hedley Verity, having taken 64 wickets at 12.42 in his debut season of 1930, was gradually becoming established as the latest in Yorkshire's distinguished line of left-arm spinners. Although this game was to be only his fourteenth appearance in the Championship and he had just taken 7 for 77 against Essex, these facts would pale into insignificance when measured against his second-day performance in this match.

Warwickshire began on a lifeless pitch under leaden skies and were reasonably well placed at 145 for 3 but the last seven wickets fell for only 56 runs. Three batsmen made useful contributions, and Canon John Parsons impressed with some powerful drives, but seven of the line-up did not even manage to get into double figures, thanks mainly to George Macaulay and Verity. Percy Holmes and Herbert Sutcliffe saw Yorkshire through to 83 for 0 by the close without any alarms.

The second day started chilly and damp with the pitch still dead but the openers, in front of 4,000 spectators, completed their fifty-ninth century opening stand for Yorkshire, scoring 120 in 100 minutes, before Edgar Oldroyd gave the innings further impetus. The home side must have felt that they needed to be in a hurry because captain Frank Greenwood scored 30 in half an hour and Arthur Wood batted boisterously as Yorkshire gained a useful lead of 97.

Hedley Verity took the first of his two instances of ten wickets in an innings at Leeds in Warwickshire's second innings.

The roller that was then used brought some moisture to the surface and, as the sun came out for the first time in the match, produced the sort of conditions that slow bowlers dream of. Bill Bowes caused one to rear nastily and, with the score on only 16, Greenwood turned to his spinners. Almost immediately he himself took a catch at mid-on to dismiss Alfred Croom off Verity's second ball. Wyatt struck the same bowler for a six in his third over but his subtle changes of flight teased the batsman incessantly. By the time Verity bowled his seventh over, Wyatt was becoming impatient and when he hit out again, with the score on 33, Holmes took the catch in the covers.

For the rest of the innings, the Warwickshire batsmen were surrounded by a cordon of close catchers and could only prod and poke at deliveries that snorted wickedly from a length. Arthur Mitchell athletically snaffled three victims at backward point, just four yards from the bat, as Verity imparted exactly the right amount of spin for the conditions.

Macaulay strove to take his first wicket and Verity dived at short-leg only to drop the ball and tear the skin on his arm. He was patched up and, in due course, his sixteenth over produced four wickets.

YORKSHIRE v. WARWICKSHIRE

John Smart was caught at backward point from the first ball, Derek Foster was stumped off the second, Cecil Tate adjudged lbw from the fifth and George Paine could only give the grateful bowler a return left-handed catch from the last. One wicket remained. After three tense overs, William Hill snicked a catch to the 'keeper and Verity had taken only the second 'ten-for' in Yorkshire's history. The game ended at 6.00p.m. with the home side having no need to bat again. Verity, still to receive his county cap, had conceded only 36 runs, exactly half the innings total.

For Verity, the remarkable events took place on his twenty-sixth birthday. With an innings analysis of 5 for 54 in the next game against Lancashire, he had begun the Championship campaign with 27 wickets in three matches at an average of 9.52. His eventual total of 138 at 12.34 was a major factor in Yorkshire regaining the title for the first time for six years and it introduced a period of unprecedented success.

YORKSHIRE v. WARWICKSHIRE

Warwickshire won the toss and elected to bat

Umpires: W. Bestwick and J.H. King

WARWICKSHIRE

R.E.S. Wyatt*	b Macaulay	13	c Holmes b Verity	23
A.J.W. Croom	c Wood b Robinson	46	c Greenwood b Verity	7
L.T.A. Bates	c Mitchell b Bowes	54	c Mitchell b Verity	19
N. Kilner	lbw b Macaulay	9	c Mitchell b Verity	0
Rev J.H. Parsons	lbw b Macaulay	48	c Leyland b Verity	9
W.A. Hill	lbw b Bowes	0	c Wood b Verity	8
J.A. Smart+	b Verity	6	c Mitchell b Verity	0
D.G. Foster	b Macaulay	5	st Wood b Verity	0
C.F. Tate	lbw b Verity	8	lbw b Verity	0
G.A.E. Paine	b Verity	6	c&b Verity	0
J.H. Mayer	not out	2	not out	6
Extras	(lb3 w1)	4		0
TOTAL		201		72

FOW 1st: 43, 67, 100, 145, 145, 176, 181, 186, 198, 201
FOW 2nd: 16, 33, 33, 51, 59, 59, 59, 59, 59, 72

Bowling: 1st: Bowes 14-5-25-2 Robinson 20-8-50-1 Macaulay 35-14-61-4 Verity 32.3-11-61-3

Bowling: 2nd: Bowes 5-1-7-0 Robinson 4-1-9-0 Verity 18.4-6-36-10 Macaulay 18-11-20-0

YORKSHIRE

P. Holmes	b Mayer	58
H. Sutcliffe	c Croom b Tate	67
M. Leyland	c Kilner b Mayer	2
E. Oldroyd	lbw b Mayer	67
A. Mitchell	b Wyatt	12
F.E. Greenwood*	c Smart b Mayer	30
E. Robinson	run out	2
A. Wood	not out	40
G.G. Macaulay	b Mayer	0
H. Verity	b Mayer	7
W.E. Bowes	c Kilner b Paine	0
Extras	(b2 lb10 nb1)	13
TOTAL		298

FOW 1st: 120, 126, 139, 182, 230, 239, 267, 271, 297, 298

Bowling: 1st: Mayer 30-8-76-6 Foster 17-2-58-0 Wyatt 8-3-12-1 Paine 17.3-3-45-1 Tate 25-6-94-1

YORKSHIRE WON BY AN INNINGS AND 25 RUNS

ESSEX v. YORKSHIRE

Date: 15, 16, 17 June 1932   County Championship
Location: Leyton

Jack Brown and John Tunnicliffe's record opening stand of 554, which had stood since 1898, was eclipsed by yet another celebrated Yorkshire pairing at Leyton. The highest and most memorable of Percy Holmes' and Herbert Sutcliffe's seventy-four century partnerships (exceeding their previous best of 347 against Hampshire in 1920) was compiled at a rate of 75 runs per hour and concluded with confusion and contention.

Brian Sellers won the toss for Yorkshire and on a pitch 'as true and easy as it could possibly be...' had no hesitation in sending Holmes and Sutcliffe to the middle. On the easy-paced and fast-scoring surface the pair made over a hundred runs in each session of play: 113 by lunch, 237 by tea and 423 unbeaten at the close. According to *Wisden*, the Yorkshire pair 'made their runs in admirable style'. This was the seventieth century partnership by the two batsmen. Holmes was 180 not out overnight, Sutcliffe, having registered his ninety-seventh first-class century (his fourth in 1932), had reached 231 including 110 in the final session of play. Holmes, who struggled with lumbago during his innings, was missed by wicket-keeper James Sheffield when the total was just four!

Despite obvious weariness and in front of a now large, expectant Leyton crowd, the opening pair continued their stand on the second morning. On 245, Sutcliffe reached his 1,000 runs for the season and this was his seventh three-figure innings against Essex. It was he who struck the two boundaries to claim the new record and he dragged the next ball onto his wicket having made 313 (his career best) including 1 six, one five and 33 fours. Sellers declared immediately. Holmes was unbeaten on 224 (his twelfth and final innings over 200), including 19 fours when the innings was closed.

Total chaos then reigned as arguments raged as to whether the stand had ended on 555 or 554; both were reported as correct. Eager photographers snapped the record-breaking duo beneath the 555 scoreboard before, 'in a dreadful silence', the board suddenly changed to 554. Fresh photographs were taken and scorecards printed as a frantic appeal went out to the scorers. Billy Ringrose (Yorkshire's scorer) told a local newspaper reporter that it was the man in the Leyton score-box that alerted them to the missing no-ball; he had recorded two, the scorers only one. Ringrose hastily sought out 'Tiger' Smith, the umpire, who confirmed he had called two no-balls. Corrections were duly made and the record finally acclaimed. The missing no-ball (apparently off the bowling of Arthur Daer) that finally confirmed the

Sutcliffe cuts a ball during the 555 opening partnership with Holmes.

new record stand remains a subject for debate even today. Their partnership lasted 465 minutes. Essex used eight bowlers in all, three of whom (Morris Nichols, Daer and Peter Smith) went for over 100 runs apiece.

On a still-perfect track, the demoralised home side were bowled out for 78 in an hour and fifty minutes. Bill Bowes took a wicket with the third ball of the innings and Hedley Verity, after a wicket with his first delivery, took five for eight in 42 balls. Following on 477 behind, Essex were overwhelmed by lunch on the third day. Nichols made 59 not out (1 six and 6 fours), the only Essex batsman to pass fifty in the match, as Bowes 'with pace off the pitch' and Verity (match figures of 10 for 53) shared the wickets in a thumping innings and 313-run victory by Yorkshire.

ESSEX v. YORKSHIRE

Yorkshire won the toss and elected to bat

Umpires: E.J. Smith and E.F. Field

YORKSHIRE

P. Holmes	not out	224
H. Sutcliffe	b Eastman	313
A. Mitchell		
M. Leyland		
W. Barber		
A.B. Sellers*		
A. Wood+		
A.C. Rhodes		
G.G. Macaulay		
H. Verity		
W.E. Bowes		
Extras	(b13 lb3 nb2)	18
TOTAL	(1 wkt dec)	555

FOW 1st: 555

Bowling 1st: Nichols 31-4-105-0 Daer 40-8-106-0 Smith 46-10-128-0 O'Connor 23-5-73-0 Eastman 22.4-2-97-1 Crawley 3-0-7-0 Taylor 4-0-14-0 Bray 1-0-7-0

ESSEX

L.G. Crawley	b Bowes	0	c Sutcliffe b Bowes	27
D.F. Pope	c Rhodes b Bowes	6	c Mitchell b Bowes	9
J. O'Connor	b Bowes	20	c Rhodes b Bowes	7
J.A. Cutmore	lbw b Bowes	0	b Verity	1
M.S. Nichols	b Verity	25	not out	59
L.C. Eastman	c Sutcliffe b Macaulay	16	c Barber b Verity	19
C. Bray*	c&b Verity	1	st Wood b Verity	6
R.M. Taylor	c Macaulay b Verity	5	c Macaulay b Verity	13
J.R. Sheffield+	c&b Verity	0	c Sutcliffe b Verity	5
A.G. Daer	c&b Verity	0	c Verity b Bowes	0
T.P.B. Smith	not out	2	c Rhodes b Bowes	0
Extras	(b3)	3	(b15 lb1 nb2)	18
TOTAL		78		164

FOW 1st: 0, 19, 19, 48, 59, 60, 66, 72, 74, 78
FOW 2nd: 38, 47, 50, 50, 92, 128, 148, 162, 164, 164

Bowling 1st: Bowes 12-1-38-4 Rhodes 10-5-15-0 Macaulay 7.1-2-14-1 Verity 7-3-8-5

Bowling 2nd: Bowes 23.4-5-47-5 Rhodes 9-5-23-0 Verity 30-12-45-5 Macaulay 16-5-31-0

YORKSHIRE WON BY AN INNINGS AND 313 RUNS

YORKSHIRE v. GLOUCESTERSHIRE

Date: 6, 7, 8 July 1932   County Championship

Location: Bradford

This match was full of runs from start to finish, featured a significant personal milestone for one of its most notable participants and concluded in a gripping manner. Yorkshire, having won the title in the previous season, were again challenging strongly and had won six (including three by an innings) and drawn two of their last eight games.

In excellent conditions for batting, Holmes and Sutcliffe put together their sixty-sixth century opening partnership for Yorkshire but both were dismissed in the 80s, the latter being caught in the slips. This merely paved the way for Arthur Mitchell who played a fine innings, putting on 136 for the fourth wicket with Wilf Barber in only ninety minutes, and remained not out when the declaration came.

Gloucestershire, not to be outdone, replied with two centuries mounting a second-wicket stand of 191. Wally Hammond, then regarded as the second-best batsman in the world after Don Bradman, played magnificently in scoring 147 in only 130 minutes and hitting 6 sixes – including some into the football stand – and 18 fours. Reggie Sinfield almost matched him stroke-for-stroke but after their partnership had ended only Charles Dacre was able to maintain the momentum. He put on 88 with Hammond and helped take the visitors past 400.

Quick runs were now needed for Yorkshire and Sutcliffe led the charge. He had scored his ninety-ninth first-class century just two weeks earlier but played here with the needs of the side uppermost in his mind. So intent was he on putting bat to ball that he expected to be out 'almost every over' and was genuinely surprised on reaching three figures. He was the seventh player to score 100 centuries, at the age of thirty-seven the youngest, and it had taken him only 700 innings – another record. His eventual total of 132,

Herbert Sutcliffe (left) and Arthur Mitchell go out to bat against Lancashire in 1936. Four years earlier the pair made centuries for the county (Sutcliffe's 100th in first-class cricket) in the victory over Gloucestershire at Bradford.

scored in the 115 minutes that the whole innings took, contained 8 sixes and 8 fours, Morris Leyland putting on 107 with him for the second wicket. So enterprising was Yorkshire's batting that, when the declaration came, they had scored their runs at a rate of 125 per hour and 5.54 per over.

All of this excitement was then cast aside in the search for victory on a wearing pitch. Gloucestershire's target of 309 in 195 minutes was merely academic and, as all collapsed around him, it seemed that only Hammond stood in the way of victory. Both George Macaulay and Hedley Verity found sufficient turn to chip away at the batting but Hammond, playing a defiant innings in complete contrast to his earlier attacking knock, constantly stood in the way.

Last man in was Tom Goddard and he played a straight bat for several overs as Hammond entrusted him to take the bowling. The former was due to take the last over and Brian Sellers, deputising for Greenwood, made a bold move to bring back Bill Bowes. The gamble worked to perfection as, to the first ball of the over, Goddard was

YORKSHIRE v. GLOUCESTERSHIRE

beaten by the extra pace and his off-stump was knocked back for Yorkshire to win an exhilarating contest. They had taken five wickets in the final half-hour and the game had concluded at 6.28p.m.

Yorkshire eventually won the Championship easily, winning five matches more than their nearest rivals. For Sutcliffe, it was the best season of his career; in all first-class matches he scored 3,336 runs at 74.13 and his Championship tally of 2,624 (at 87.46) still stands as the record for Yorkshire, being over 400 runs more than that of his nearest rival. But he would never forget his personal goal in an exciting match at Bradford.

YORKSHIRE v. GLOUCESTERSHIRE

Yorkshire won the toss and elected to bat

Umpires: J.H. King and W.R. Parry

YORKSHIRE

P. Holmes	c Dacre b Hammond	81	c Watkins b Rogers	2
H. Sutcliffe	c Hammond b Rogers	83	c Barnett b Parker	132
A. Mitchell	not out	177	lbw b Goddard	9
M. Leyland	c Hammond b Goddard	3	c Sinfield b Goddard	58
W. Barber	c Lyon b Neale	62	(6) c Barnett b Parker	10
A.B. Sellers*	b Sinfield	12	(5) c Allen b Parker	0
A. Wood	run out	17	(7) not out	4
W. Rhodes	b Sinfield	6		
H. Verity	not out	14		
G.G. Macaulay				
W.E. Bowes				
Extras	(b11 lb6)	17	(b9 lb16)	25
TOTAL	(7 wkts dec)	472	(6 wkts dec)	240

FOW 1st: 161, 173, 178, 314, 355, 418, 447
FOW 2nd: 8, 57, 164, 170, 184, 240

Bowling: 1st: Rogers 16-1-53-1 Hammond 29-4-89-1 Goddard 50-14-121-1 Parker 45-16-97-0
Sinfield 16-4-40-2 Barnett 4-0-15-0 Lyon 3-0-19-0 Neale 3-0-21-1

Bowling 2nd: Rogers 5-0-13-1 Hammond 4-1-27-0 Parker 12.2-1-81-3 Goddard 11-1-58-2
Sinfield 11-2-36-0

GLOUCESTERSHIRE

R.A. Sinfield	c Wood b Macaulay	110	b Macaulay	36
C.J. Barnett	b Rhodes	8	lbw b Macaulay	16
W.R. Hammond	c Rhodes b Bowes	147	(6) not out	71
W.L. Neale	c Mitchell b Bowes	1	(3) b Macaulay	2
B.O. Allen	c Bowes b Macaulay	1	(4) c Mitchell b Verity	0
B.H. Lyon*	b Macaulay	17	(7) lbw b Macaulay	10
C.C.R. Dacre	not out	71	(5) b Macaulay	27
J.A. Rogers	b Macaulay	19	c Sutcliffe b Verity	1
B.T.L. Watkins+	c Macaulay b Verity	0	b Verity	0
T.W.J. Goddard	run out	7	(11) b Bowes	0
C.W.L. Parker	c Sutcliffe b Verity	8	(10) b Verity	0
Extras	(b11 lb4)	15	(b7 lb4 nb1)	12
TOTAL		404		175

FOW 1st: 9, 200, 218, 225, 258, 346, 380, 383, 394, 404
FOW 2nd: 50, 56, 58, 144, 158, 172, 173, 173, 175, 175

Bowling 1st: Bowes 33-4-137-2 Rhodes 24-5-50-1 Macaulay 35-7-103-4 Verity 22.2-3-96-2
Leyland 3-1-3-0

Bowling 2nd: Bowes 14.1-2-41-1 Macaulay 28-10-67-5 Verity 20-8-54-4 Rhodes 2-1-1-0

YORKSHIRE WON BY 133 RUNS

YORKSHIRE v. NOTTINGHAMSHIRE

Date: 9, 11, 12 July 1932   County Championship
Location: Headingley

Hedley Verity, Yorkshire's successor to Wilfred Rhodes as the side's slow left-arm bowler, had already demonstrated his impressive credentials to the cricketing public the previous season, having made his county debut in 1930. His tally of 188 first-class wickets in 1931 not only brought him his England cap but also included an analysis of 10 for 36 in an innings against Warwickshire, the first of two such career achievements. The second and most remarkable of these took place in this county match against Nottinghamshire.

Yorkshire's 1932 season took a long while to gather any serious momentum. May brought only one Championship victory (over Somerset at Bath), heavy defeat against Lancashire in the Roses match at Bradford, two matches abandoned without a ball bowled versus Derbyshire and Kent and a draw with Warwickshire. The second (and last) Championship defeat of 1932 came in the opening fixture of June – Hampshire beating them at Headingley by 49 runs. After another draw in the return match with Warwickshire, Yorkshire's fortunes were transformed. In the remainder of that month they won five and drew two of their seven games.

Amateur batsman Brian Sellers (son of the former Yorkshire player Arthur Sellers) made his debut in 1932 and found himself with the captaincy for the majority of the season as the incumbent Frank Greenwood was only available for six matches due to business commitments. Sellers made an immediate impact. He scored almost 700 Championship runs and led Yorkshire to eighteen victories. However, on the morning of Saturday 9 July 1932 he lost the toss to his counterpart Arthur Carr, and Nottinghamshire chose to bat first on a somewhat green and moist pitch, having arrived at Headingley on the back of three comfortable wins against Gloucestershire, All India and Worcestershire.

The visitors made a poor start to their innings. Openers Walter Keeton and Frank Shipston made nine and eight respectively, skipper Carr was well caught on the boundary off a Verity half volley without troubling the scorers and Arthur Staples managed only three before being bowled by George Macaulay. That left Nottinghamshire 46 for 4, which soon became 67 for 5 just after lunch when Walker was caught by Barber. However, the Nottinghamshire's middle-order provided some stout resistance. Wicketkeeper Ben Lilley remained 46 not out (including five crisp fours) whilst fast bowler Harold Larwood, batting at no.9, top scored with 48, including 1 six, off Verity and 4 fours. The innings might have been even more imposing had Morris Leyland not taken three clean-bowled wickets in eight balls for no runs with his left-arm 'chinaman' bowling. He finished with figures of 4 for 14 and the first day's play ended with Nottinghamshire 234 all out.

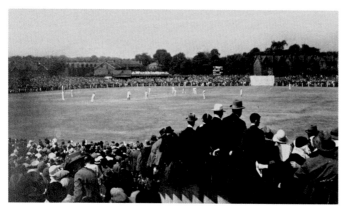

Headingley – scene of Verity's world-record innings analysis in first-class cricket.

YORKSHIRE v. NOTTINGHAMSHIRE

Hedley Verity (left) pictured at The Oval in August 1932 alongside Herbert Sutcliffe and Morris Leyland (right). The trio, together with Bill Bowes (emerging from the pavilion behind Arthur Mitchell), were all chosen in the MCC party that toured Australia that winter in what became known as the Bodyline series of 1932/33.

The Yorkshire reply on the second morning ran into immediate trouble when Larwood removed Herbert Sutcliffe caught by Voce at third slip for a duck. Arthur Mitchell was hit on the hand by Larwood when his score was 11 and didn't return until the score had reached 125 for 5. Percy Holmes proved the major obstacle for Larwood and Bill Voce. His 65 included 7 fours and he batted for just short of two and a quarter hours before Larwood finally bowled him. Yorkshire were 163 for 9 when thunderstorms brought an end to proceedings at 3.55p.m. Larwood's five wickets had cost him 73 runs from 22 hostile overs and Nottinghamshire held a significant first-innings advantage.

Play finally got underway at 12.30p.m. on the third day and, mindful of the conditions, Sellers immediately declared the Yorkshire innings at their overnight total, 71 runs behind Nottinghamshire. The openers Keeton and Shipston dug in for what they hoped would be a long stay and having batted with great care they went to lunch at 38 without loss. Another rain-ruined draw seemed likely as the afternoon session got underway. Before lunch, Verity had bowled seven consecutive maidens and his first two overs after the interval continued that theme. Off the third ball of the third, Shipston took two. That was followed by another maiden before Verity broke the partnership when Keeton (21) was caught at slip from the first ball of his fifth over. Shipston was caught at the wicket three runs later, also for 21. Nottinghamshire's captain Carr completed his pair (one of three Nottinghamshire batsmen dismissed twice without scoring in the match) attempting to hit Verity for six, caught by Wilf Barber for the second time in the match just in front of the sightscreen. Willis Walker and Staples added 12 together for the fourth wicket. Verity's eleventh over in this phenomenal spell brought him his first hat-trick.

Willis Walker, brilliantly caught at slip by Macaulay, was the first victim; Charlie Harris was caught by Holmes at backward point; and George Gunn was lbw to a straight ball. Staples took a single off Macaulay at the other end. Macaulay refused to bowl wide of the crease despite the realisation that Verity had a chance of taking all ten wickets. Staples fell to Verity in his twelfth over and Larwood lofted a catch to Sutcliffe running back at extra cover; Nottinghamshire 64 for 8.

A second Verity hat-trick was an unimaginable possibility in his next over but Lilley edged the ball for three. Voce lasted two balls and Sam Staples became Verity's tenth scalp when Arthur Wood stumped him off the next delivery. Verity's last three overs read (.www..), (....ww), (3.ww). His final figures of 10 for 10 remain the world-record innings analysis for all first-class cricket. The ten wickets were taken in the space of 52 balls and he ended the innings with a spell of 7 in 15 balls and 4 in 6. He conceded the ten runs in four overs; the other seven he bowled after lunch were maidens. All but one of his ten victims had made a first-class century. The ten wickets had fallen in the space of sixty-five minutes for 23 runs. Strangely, during both of his ten-wicket feats, against Nottinghamshire in this match and Warwickshire the previous season, not once did he hit the stumps and the actual mode of dismissals exactly tallied; eight of the batsmen were caught; one stumped and the other lbw!

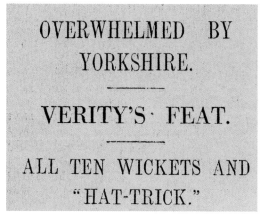

OVERWHELMED BY YORKSHIRE.

VERITY'S · FEAT.

ALL TEN WICKETS AND "HAT-TRICK."

Above: This Nottingham newspaper headline proclaims Verity's spectacular bowling feat.

Left: Brian Sellers – Yorkshire debutant in 1932 and captain for the bulk of the season. His overnight declaration enabled Verity to wreak havoc on the third afternoon.

YORKSHIRE v. NOTTINGHAMSHIRE

Such was the speed of Verity's massacre that Yorkshire required 139 to win in 165 minutes. Holmes (77 not out with 9 fours) and Sutcliffe (54 not out) took only ninety minutes of the allocated time to reach their target and thus record the county's fourth consecutive victory. As Yorkshire moved to the top of the Championship placings for the first time in 1932, hundreds of spectators queued for Verity's autograph on the souvenir scorecards hastily printed to celebrate a unique moment in the Club's history.

YORKSHIRE v. NOTTINGHAMSHIRE

Nottinghamshire won the toss and elected to bat

Umpires: H.G. Baldwin and W. Reeves

NOTTINGHAMSHIRE

W.W. Keeton	b Rhodes	9	c Macaulay b Verity	21
F.W. Shipston	b Macaulay	8	c Wood b Verity	21
W. Walker	c Barber b Bowes	36	c Macaulay b Verity	11
A.W. Carr*	c Barber b Verity	0	c Barber b Verity	0
A. Staples	b Macaulay	3	c Macaulay b Verity	7
C.B. Harris	lbw b Leyland	35	c Holmes b Verity	0
G.V. Gunn	b Verity	31	lbw b Verity	0
B. Lilley+	not out	46	not out	3
H. Larwood	b Leyland	48	c Sutcliffe b Verity	0
W. Voce	b Leyland	0	c Holmes b Verity	0
S.J. Staples	b Leyland	0	st Wood b Verity	0
Extras	(b8 lb6 w2 nb2)	18	(b3 nb1)	4
TOTAL		234		67

FOW 1st: 15, 35, 40, 46, 67, 120, 159, 233, 233, 234
FOW 2nd: 44, 47, 51, 63, 63, 63, 64, 64, 67, 67

Bowling 1st: Bowes 31-9-55-1 Rhodes 28-8-49-1 Verity 41-13-64-2 Macaulay 24-10-34-2 Leyland 8.2-3-14-4

Bowling 2nd: Bowes 5-0-19-0 Macaulay 23-9-34-0 Verity 19.4-16-10-10

YORKSHIRE

P. Holmes	b Larwood	65	not out	77
H. Sutcliffe	c Voce b Larwood	0	not out	54
A. Mitchell	run out	24		
M. Leyland	b Voce	5		
W. Barber	c&b Larwood	34		
A.B. Sellers*	b A. Staples	0		
A. Wood+	b Larwood	1		
A.C. Rhodes	c A. Staples b Voce	3		
H. Verity	b Larwood	12		
G.G. Macaulay	not out	8		
W.E. Bowes	not out	1		
Extras	(b5 lb5)	10	(b4 lb4)	8
TOTAL	(9 wkts dec)	163	(0 wkts)	139

FOW 1st: 1, 37, 122, 123, 125, 128, 135, 152, 154

Bowling 1st: Larwood 22-4-73-5 Voce 22-2-52-2 S.J. Staples 7-2-8-0 A. Staples 11-3-20-1

Bowling 2nd: Larwood 3-0-14-0 Voce 10-0-43-0 S.J. Staples 18.4-5-37-0 A. Staples 6-1-25-0 Harris 3-0-12-0

YORKSHIRE WON BY TEN WICKETS

ESSEX v. YORKSHIRE

Date: 12, 13, 14 July 1933   County Championship
Location: Leyton

Having witnessed a remarkable batting feat in 1932, Leyton's spectators were to see, for the next visit of Yorkshire, an equally astounding masterpiece of bowling. The visitors arrived having won six of their last eight matches (including four by an innings) and were intent on completing a hat-trick of Championship titles.

As in 1932, Yorkshire lost the toss and were asked to bat, but there the similarities end. With Yorkshire's score on 76 for 3, Charles Bray's decision to field looked a good one. Arthur Mitchell and Wilf Barber set about repairing the damage but Mitchell, having reached 43, was struck by a ball on the left temple and had to retire hurt. The score stuttered to 138 for 5 but Barber was still at the crease and he found willing allies in Hedley Verity and Arthur Wood who helped him put on stands of 60 and 97 respectively.

Although Mitchell was unable to resume his innings, so well did the tail wag that 202 runs were put on for the last four wickets. Barber passed three figures and was at the crease for just over three and a half hours. He had fought well through the early stages of the day when batting had been difficult and enabled Yorkshire to benefit when the pitch eased during the afternoon. Essex reached 13 without loss by the close of play.

The whole of the second day's play was lost due to rain and the man most disappointed was Jack O'Connor, whose benefit match this was. When it came to the final day, however, it was the whole of the Essex team who were disappointed as they lost 20 wickets for 155 runs. No less than 17 of these were taken by Verity, for 91 runs, as he equalled the feat of Colin Blythe, also a left-arm spinner, who had taken 17 wickets in a day in 1907.

The previous day's rain had affected the pitch considerably; it was soft and there was also a strong wind and a warm sun to dry it. The ball did not spin as viciously as expected but popped and reared at unexpected heights. The Essex batsmen were completely baffled and Brian Sellers benefited to the tune of five catches as well as running out Dudley Pope. The latter made the top score of both innings in batting for two hours with care and resolution and also sharing Essex's highest stand of 39 with O'Connor. Verity and George Macauley shared 49 of the 58 overs bowled in the first innings.

Wilf Barber scored a faultless hundred on day one before Hedley Verity claimed 17 wickets on the rain-damaged Leyton pitch on day three.

Essex's second innings began worse than their first as they lost their first four wickets for only ten runs. Verity added to his eight earlier wickets by taking a further nine with the persevering Macaulay taking the other. The innings lasted only 28.1 overs – less than half the length of the first knock and the game even finished before four o'clock – an amazing day.

This match came as the second in a sequence of fine performances for Verity. In the previous game he had figures of 13 for 102 and in the next two took 9 for 153 and 11 for 92 – a total of 50 wickets at an average of 8.76. Not only that, he had now taken 50 wickets against Essex in his first three seasons, including 36 at Leyton at 6.94. He was to top the national averages for the whole season and then, in 1934, have his finest hour as an international player when his 14 wickets in a day would ensure that Australia were beaten at Lord's for what came to be the only time in the twentieth century.

ESSEX v. YORKSHIRE

Essex won the toss and elected to field

Umpires: J.A. Newman and J. Stone

YORKSHIRE

P. Holmes	c Sheffield b Smith	15
H. Sutcliffe	b Evans	36
A. Mitchell	retired hurt	43
M. Leyland	lbw b Smith	3
W. Barber	b Smith	101
A.B. Sellers*	c O'Connor b Smith	1
F. Dennis	c Daer b Smith	6
H. Verity	c Smith b Evans	28
A. Wood	b Nichols	85
G.G. Macaulay	c Cutmore b Nichols	2
W. Rhodes	not out	9
Extras	(b8 lb3)	11
TOTAL		340

FOW 1st: 35, 71, 76, 123, 138, 198, 295, 320, 340

Bowling 1st: Nichols 20.4-3-59-2 Daer 15-3-40-0 Smith 45-9-122-5 Evans 31-7-69-2 Boswell 4-0-15-0 O'Connor 13-4-24-0

ESSEX

J.A. Cutmore	c Sellers b Verity	3	c Dennis b Verity	6
D.F. Pope	run out	34	c Sutcliffe b Verity	0
R.M. Taylor	c Sellers b Verity	0	b Verity	2
J. O'Connor	c Sutcliffe b Verity	17	lbw b Macaulay	0
M.S. Nichols	b Verity	4	c Sellers b Verity	4
C. Bray*	lbw b Verity	2	c Barber b Verity	14
J.R. Sheffield+	c Barber b Verity	9	b Verity	7
A.G. Daer	c Sellers b Leyland	3	not out	13
T.P.B. Smith	c Sellers b Verity	11	c Sellers b Verity	15
C.S.R. Boswell	not out	2	c Dennis b Verity	0
V.J. Evans	c Sellers b Verity	0	st Wood b Verity	0
Extras	(b8 lb11)	19	(lb3)	3
TOTAL		104		64

FOW 1st: 19, 19, 58, 69, 76, 76, 87, 95, 104, 104
FOW 2nd: 1, 3, 4, 10, 26, 31, 34, 52, 52, 64

Bowling 1st: Macaulay 22-9-25-0 Sellers 1-0-5-0 Verity 27-10-47-8 Rhodes 5-5-0-0 Leyland 3-1-8-1

Bowling 2nd: Verity 14.1-3-44-9 Macaulay 11-5-12-1 Leyland 3-1-5-0

YORKSHIRE WON BY AN INNINGS AND 172 RUNS

YORKSHIRE v. DERBYSHIRE

Date: 24, 26, 27 June 1939   County Championship

Location: Bramall Lane, Sheffield

Yorkshire's penultimate pre-war county fixture with Derbyshire in the summer of 1939 was a match of several significant highs and lows, with the bowlers on both sides dominant for all but one crucial period of the game.

Play at Bramall Lane didn't get under way until 2.30p.m. on the first day (Saturday) due to rain. No time was lost in the progress of the game, despite the poor weather, as 20 wickets fell for only 103 runs in just under three and three-quarter hours on that opening afternoon. The pitch was firmer underneath than anyone expected, and this made the ball 'lift and fly off the damp surface in the most alarming manner' as Yorkshire, having won the toss, managed only 83 all out in their first innings. This was their lowest score for three years. Captain Brian Sellers top scored with 31 as the Pope brothers (Alf and George) claimed all 10 home team wickets in conditions ideal for swing bowling. The Derbyshire reply was calamitous. Their entire innings lasted only forty-four minutes and 67 balls. Twenty all out was their second-lowest score ever, beaten only by their 16 against Nottingham in 1879. It was also the lowest county score for seventeen years (Hampshire made 22 in 1922). Colt Jim Smurthwaite (a fast-medium bowler from North Ormesby allocated to Sheffield United for the 1939 season) was opening the bowling for Yorkshire for the first time in the absence of Bill Bowes (Test duty), and had the stunning figures of 5 for 7 from four completed overs. By the close of an unforgettable day, Yorkshire were 13 for no wicket in their second innings.

Frank Smailes – Yorkshire's third bowler to take all ten wickets in an innings in a first-class match.

Wickets continued to tumble on the second day, 14 in total, but runs came Yorkshire's way in equal measure thanks largely to Wilf Barber who registered his first century of the season and, in doing so, was also the only player in the match to pass 50. His hundred included 14 fours and he shared valuable middle-order partnerships with Norman Yardley, George Wilson and Sellers. Derbyshire were left an unlikely victory target of 374 to win. Frank Smailes, bowling 'with real fire', set about dismantling the visitors' second innings. His excellent length and medium-paced swingers had already accounted for four Derbyshire batsmen by the time close of play was called on day two with only 31 runs on the board. The single-handed demolition continued on the final morning. Three wickets fell in the first half-hour. Alf Pope was bowled with 'a magnificent out-swinger' whilst Gladwin's leg stump was sent flying with an equally deadly in-swinger. Only Stan Worthington, with 32, stood firm for Derbyshire before being brilliantly caught one-handed by Mitchell. Smailes became the third Yorkshire bowler

YORKSHIRE v. DERBYSHIRE

in first-class cricket (after Alonzo Drake and Hedley Verity) to take all ten wickets in an innings. The game ended at 12.15p.m. with Derbyshire comprehensively vanquished by 276 runs. Smailes' match figures of 14 for 58 were a career-best return. All eleven Derbyshire batsmen were included in his 14 wickets across the two innings, having bowled unchanged throughout the match. An ankle operation the previous winter hindered Smailes' form in 1939 and he was destined to lose possibly some of his best years to the Second World War. However, the North Yorkshire all-rounder certainly left behind the final pre-war summer with a performance to cherish from this match with Derbyshire.

YORKSHIRE v. DERBYSHIRE

Yorkshire won the toss and elected to bat

Umpires: H.G. Baldwin and H. Elliott

YORKSHIRE

H. Sutcliffe	c Worthington b A.V. Pope	9	c Gladwin b G.H. Pope	18
A. Mitchell	c Rhodes b G.H. Pope	14	c Smith b A.V. Pope	40
W. Barber	c Elliott b A.V. Pope	2	c Smith b A.V. Pope	100
M. Leyland	b G.H. Pope	0	c Elliott b G.H. Pope	1
N.W.D. Yardley	c Gladwin b A.V. Pope	21	c&b Rhodes	34
G.A. Wilson	b A.V. Pope	0	b Mitchell	21
A.B. Sellers*	c Elliott b G.H. Pope	31	run out	43
T.F. Smailes	c A.V. Pope b G.H. Pope	4	b A.V. Pope	8
E.P. Robinson	b G.H. Pope	0	c Hounsfield b G.H. Pope	23
J. Smurthwaite	b G.H. Pope	0	b A.V. Pope	1
K. Fiddling+	not out	0	not out	5
Extras	(lb2)	2	(b8 lb8)	16
TOTAL		83		310

FOW 1st: 20, 26, 26, 31, 32, 63, 70, 70, 70, 83
FOW 2nd: 45, 76, 77, 140, 189, 260, 281, 284, 290, 310

Bowling 1st: A.V. Pope 18-4-37-4 G.H. Pope 17.3-2-44-6

Bowling 2nd: A.V. Pope 25-5-72-4 G.H. Pope 24.5-3-90-3 Mitchell 9-0-52-1 Gladwin 8-2-36-0 Rhodes 4-0-16-1 Townsend 5-0-28-0

DERBYSHIRE

D. Smith	b Smurthwaite	5	b Smailes	8
A.E. Alderman	c Fidding b Smailes	1	c Smurthwaite b Smailes	0
T.S. Worthington	run out	0	c Mitchell b Smailes	32
L.F. Townsend	c Robinson b Smurthwaite	2	b Smailes	0
G.H. Pope	c Robinson b Smailes	0	lbw b Smailes	1
A.E.G. Rhodes	c Robinson b Smurthwaite	0	b Smailes	18
T.D. Hounsfield*	c Sutcliffe b Smailes	2	not out	21
A.V. Pope	b Smurthwaite	6	b Smailes	4
C. Gladwin	c Smailes b Smurthwaite	0	b Smailes	0
H. Elliott+	not out	2	b Smailes	6
T.B. Mitchell	c Leyland b Smailes	0	st Fiddling b Smailes	6
Extras	(lb2)	2	(b1)	1
TOTAL		20		97

FOW 1st: 2, 2, 7, 8, 10, 10, 13, 14, 19, 20
FOW 2nd: 0, 19, 19, 21, 56, 61, 71, 71, 79, 97

Bowling 1st: Smailes 4.3-0-11-4 Smurthwaite 4-2-7-5

Bowling 2nd: Smailes 17.1-5-47-10 Smurthwaite 14-5-43-0 Yardley 2-0-5-0 Robinson 1-0-1-0

YORKSHIRE WON BY 276 RUNS

SUSSEX v. YORKSHIRE

Date: 30, 31 August, 1 September 1939   County Championship
Location: Hove

This is a game that, despite the fine cricket it contained as well as some outstanding individual performances, was played in an unreal atmosphere as the whole country was preparing for war. The Scarborough Festival had been cancelled, the West Indian tourists had left with seven of their games left unplayed and, by the third day of this game, Leicester was the only other ground in the country where first-class cricket was also being played.

Yorkshire had already won the County Championship (for the seventh time in nine seasons) and were due to complete their traditional southern tour that had so far consisted of innings wins at Dover and Bournemouth. The Brighton and Hove Cricket Week should have been a gala occasion for Yorkshire's visit but the air was festered with the tension and talk of war. The band played merrily while tea was served in the marquees but the conversations were sombre. The players knew that this would be their last game for some time and tried to enjoy themselves. For similar reasons the crowd was larger than usual.

Sussex won the toss and made the highest total that Yorkshire had conceded all season. George Cox compiled a scintillating near-double century with powerful drives and elegant deflections in only 220 minutes. He was especially severe on Hedley Verity, hitting him for six over mid on, this adding to his 28 fours. Almost 500 runs were scored on the first day, Yorkshire finishing on 112 for 1.

The shortened second day's play saw Yorkshire bat on a rain-affected pitch and Len Hutton produce a masterclass on how to deal with a clever bowler on such a surface. The potentially destructive left-arm spin of Jim Langridge was negated as Hutton would not let him settle on a length. He regularly came down to meet the ball on the full and also had an appropriate answer when Langridge pitched short. The Champions concluded the day on 330 for 3, Hutton, having hit 14 fours in a flawless innings, falling to Cox with a missed sweep.

The third day started with news that Germany had invaded Poland and war was now inevitable. The Yorkshire committee suggested that the game be called off, but the players decided to continue as it was the benefit match for Jim Parks. Meanwhile, play at Leicester was abandoned and all games due to start on the following day were cancelled.

Yorkshire lost their last seven wickets for 50 runs to give them a negligible lead under a blazing sun as the pitch dried and cut up dramatically. This collapse was nothing, however, to the way in which Verity then tortured the home batsmen. It took a mere 91 balls for he and Ellis Robinson to bowl unchanged and dismiss Sussex for a paltry 33. Yorkshire knocked off the required runs carefully in 102 balls and lost only one wicket in the process. The game finished at 2.30p.m.

Yorkshire's returning coach passed cars leaving London piled up with belongings of every description

Leyland batting during the match at Hove. George Cox, who had earlier made 198, is at short leg with James Langridge at slip.

SUSSEX v. YORKSHIRE

as people fled the capital. Due to an experimental blackout, the team stayed in Leicester overnight and the final leg of the journey saw one of the greatest teams in the history of county cricket disembark one by one until it reached City Square, Leeds.

Verity's spell in the second innings had seen him take seven wickets for nine runs in only six (eight-ball) overs. The conditions were made for him and he knew exactly how to exploit them. He wondered if he would ever play there again and had no smile of success. Truth to tell, he would never play anywhere.

SUSSEX v. YORKSHIRE

Sussex won the toss and elected to bat

Umpires: J.J. Hills and C.W.L. Parker

SUSSEX

R.G. Stainton	c Wood b Bowes	14	absent injured	
J.G. Langridge	run out	60	(1) c Sellers b Robinson	3
H.W. Parks	c Wood b Smailes	35	c Hutton b Verity	9
G. Cox	c Mitchell b Robinson	198	c Wood b Verity	9
J. Langridge	c Mitchell b Bowes	17	c Mitchell b Verity	0
J.H. Parks	c Robinson b Smailes	2	(2) lbw b Verity	0
H.T. Bartlett	b Robinson	24	(6) b Verity	3
A.J. Holmes*	b Verity	11	(7) b Verity	4
S.C. Griffith+	c Smailes b Verity	17	(8) b Verity	1
J.K. Nye	not out	2	(9) not out	3
D.J. Wood	lbw b Robinson	0	(10) run out	0
Extras	(b3 lb4)	7	(b1)	1
TOTAL		387		33

FOW 1st: 26, 89, 133, 202, 205, 266, 321, 361, 387, 387
FOW 2nd: 0, 12, 12, 13, 19, 23, 25, 30, 33

Bowling 1st: Bowes 17-0-71-2 Smailes 12-0-48-2 Yardley 9-0-48-0 Verity 18-1-108-2 Robinson 15-2-87-3 Hutton 4-0-18-0

Bowling 2nd: Verity 6-1-9-7 Robinson 5.3-0-23-1

YORKSHIRE

L. Hutton	lbw b Cox	103	c Griffith b J. Langridge	1
W. Barber	c Griffith b Nye	22	not out	18
A. Mitchell	c J. Langridge b Holmes	67	not out	11
M. Leyland	c sub b J.H. Parks	64		
N.W.D. Yardley	c&b J. Langridge	108		
A.B. Sellers*	c Bartlett b J.H. Parks	12		
T.F. Smailes	b J.H. Parks	0		
A. Wood	c Wood b J. Landridge	2		
E.P. Robinson	b J. Langridge	0		
H. Verity	not out	7		
W.E. Bowes	c J.H. Parks b J. Langridge	2		
Extras	(b3 lb1 w1)	5		0
TOTAL		392	(1 wkt)	30

FOW 1st: 52, 175, 204, 342, 363, 364, 377, 377, 386, 392
FOW 2nd: 4

Bowling 1st: Nye 19-1-104-1 J.H. Parks 33-3-120-3 Wood 10-1-30-0 J. Langridge 20.4-5-84-4 Cox 10-2-34-1 Holmes 3-0-15-1

Bowling 2nd: J.H. Parks 6.6-1-21-0 J. Langridge 6-0-9-1

YORKSHIRE WON BY NINE WICKETS

YORKSHIRE v. SOMERSET

Date: 26, 28, 29 May 1951   County Championship
Location: Bramall Lane, Sheffield

Prior to this game, winning a match after following on had been achieved only three times by Yorkshire since their formation in 1863. All three victories had been in the nineteenth century (1879 *v.* Gloucestershire, 1890 *v.* Surrey and 1892 *v.* Sussex). Bramall Lane had hosted two of those matches and in 1951 the Sheffield ground was again the venue for another famous follow-on success.

Somerset were destined for a poor season. As *Wisden* (1952) commented, 'Somerset lost much of their traditional ability to spring surprises', and they dropped seven places in the Championship table, finishing fourth from bottom with only five victories registered. A rare triumph certainly seemed likely, though, two days into this tussle with Yorkshire at Sheffield. Batting first on a 'green pitch', according to the *Sheffield Telegraph*, the West Country visitors recovered from a shaky start against Bob Appleyard (who was already on his way towards 200 first-class wickets in the season) and Fred Trueman. Appleyard, in a spell of seventy-five minutes with the new ball, took two wickets for 22 runs from 12 overs. 'Exhilarating batting', by Maurice Tremlett and good support from Bertie Buse and Johnny Lawrence, who contributed useful 30s, helped raise the Somerset total to a respectable 234 all out. Appleyard and Trueman finished with three wickets apiece whilst leg-break bowler Eddie Leadbeater hastened the Somerset innings to a close with figures of 4 for 57 from 17.5 overs. Somerset lost their last four wickets for 22 runs.

Conditions on the second day (Monday), when only ninety minutes' play was possible, were very much in favour of the bowling side: 'Thick clouds hung over the ground and factory chimneys and church steeples were etched black on the skyline', recorded the local newspaper report. Yorkshire crumbled against the swing of Jim Redman and Buse, the latter ending with 6 for 33. Two years later, Buse would contribute to ruining his own benefit match taking 6 for 41 as the game against Lancashire was completed in a day! His scalps in Yorkshire's first innings included Len Hutton for nine and Frank Lowson, who top scored with 20. Following on 157 in arrears, Yorkshire's batsmen played with far greater self-assurance and enterprise on the final day. Half centuries from Hutton (his first of the season), Harry Halliday and Vic Wilson set up the opportunity for Don Brennan (leading Yorkshire in the absence of Norman Yardley, who missed the game suffering from lumbago) to declare at tea, leaving Somerset just short of two hours to chase a sporting 113 for victory.

One of the players most likely to take Somerset to their target – Harold Gimblett – went without scoring, bowled by Appleyard with the second ball of the innings. Very

Bramall Lane, Sheffield – the venue for Yorkshire's win over Somerset, despite having followed on.

quickly the run chase was in tatters. Only five runs were on the board by the time the third Somerset wicket fell. Over-aggressive batting opened the door for Yorkshire's Appleyard (bowling fast off-breaks, mixed with in-swingers to a leg trap) and, in particular, Johnny Wardle ('admirable length and lift') to exploit. Wardle's spin removed the Somerset middle-order of Eric Hill, Maurice Tremlett, Buse and Lawrence. Skipper (and at that time club secretary) Stuart Scott Rogers top scored with 19 but Yorkshire were not to be denied and in winning by 50 runs registered an unlikely hat-trick of follow-on victories at Bramall Lane with nearly half an hour to spare on the third evening.

YORKSHIRE v. SOMERSET

Somerset won the toss and elected to bat

Umpires: L.J. Todd and C.H. Welch

SOMERSET

Batsman	Dismissal 1	1st	Dismissal 2	2nd
H. Gimblett	b Appleyard	8	b Appleyard	0
F.L. Angell	b Appleyard	27	c Hutton b Appleyard	0
E. Hill	c Brennan b Trueman	3	c Hutton b Wardle	1
M.F. Tremlett	c Wardle b Leadbeater	81	st Brennan b Wardle	11
H.T.F. Buse	b Trueman	38	c Brennan b Wardle	8
J. Lawrence	not out	30	c Brennan b Wardle	0
R. Smith	b Appleyard	2	not out	0
S.S. Rogers*	c Hutton b Leadbeater	24	b Appleyard	19
H.W. Stephenson+	c Leadbeater b Trueman	3	c Brennan b Wardle	7
E.P. Robinson	lbw b Leadbeater	5	c Trueman b Wardle	4
J. Redman	b Leadbeater	10	b Leadbeater	8
Extras	(lb3)	3	(b4)	4
TOTAL		234		62

FOW 1st: 11, 28, 55, 149, 168, 171, 212, 217, 222, 234
FOW 2nd: 0, 5, 5, 31, 39, 46, 46, 48, 62, 62

Bowling 1st: Trueman 24-4-73-3 Appleyard 27-7-49-3 Halliday 9-4-16-0 Wardle 25-15-36-0 Leadbeater 17.5-2-57-4

Bowling 2nd: Appleyard 13-3-35-3 Wardle 14-6-23-6 Leadbeater 1.5-1-0-1

YORKSHIRE

Batsman	Dismissal 1	1st	Dismissal 2	2nd
L. Hutton	b Buse	9	c Stephenson b Robinson	65
F.A. Lowson	c Redman b Buse	20	st Stephenson b Lawrence	43
H. Halliday	lbw b Redman	2	c Tremlett b Buse	55
W.H.H. Sutcliffe	b Buse	10	c Tremlett b Robinson	12
J.V. Wilson	c Lawrence b Redman	16	c Stephenson b Redman	56
E.I. Lester	lbw b Buse	0	not out	5
J.H. Wardle	b Buse	7	c Stephenson b Lawrence	26
E. Leadbeater	run out	0	c Rogers b Lawrence	7
D.V. Brennan*+	b Buse	3		
R. Appleyard	not out	5		
F.S. Trueman	st Stephenson b Redman	2		
Extras	(b1 lb2)	3		
TOTAL		77	(7 wkts dec)	269

FOW 1st: 13, 15, 40, 45, 45, 67, 67, 67, 72, 77
FOW 2nd: 86, 132, 206, 226, 252, 257, 269

Bowling 1st: Redman 22.4-9-41-3 Buse 22-10-33-6

Bowling 2nd: Redman 15-3-69-1 Buse 19-5-56-1 Robinson 29-6-74-2 Lawrence 24.5-4-70-3

YORKSHIRE WON BY 50 RUNS

SURREY v. YORKSHIRE

Date: 14, 16, 17 July 1951   County Championship
Location: The Oval

The two sides involved in this game were to be strong rivals throughout the whole of the 1950s. Both teams had finished in the top five of the County Championship for each of the last three seasons. Surrey, in 1950, had been declared joint champions with Lancashire, and Yorkshire finished in third place. The visitors themselves had been joint champions with Middlesex in 1949.

However, on this occasion, there was the added interest of a significant personal milestone being reached. On 19 June, Len Hutton had scored the ninety-ninth century of his first-class career and, over the succeeding weeks, there had been continuous speculation as to when the 100th hundred might be made. A series of low scores had followed but an opportunity presented itself at Old Trafford in the third Test against South Africa. England needed only 139 to win and Hutton dominated an opening stand with Jack Ikin. Ikin, who was encouraging the master batsman on his way towards three figures by letting him take most of the bowling, made only 38 out of a partnership of 121. Despite hitting a four to win the match, England's victory came with Hutton on 98 not out – a tantalising two runs short of becoming the first player to score his 100th century in a Test match.

Hutton himself showed no particular concern and commented that the record 'barring miracles, was likely to come before the end of the season'. At one stage, Cuan McCarthy, the South African fast

bowler, had bowled 'donkey-drops' to Reg Simpson, Hutton's latter partner, so that he would score and deny Hutton the century. Simpson merely blocked the insulting deliveries. It was perhaps appropriate that Hutton did not achieve the target in such circumstances, *The Times* reporter commenting that 'pantomime was permitted to stalk the field'.

Next stop for Hutton was Hull and a county match against Sussex. His first-innings score was 23 but a last-day situation in which Yorkshire had to bat for a draw was tailor-made for him. He got to 54 out of a total of 75 for 3 but rain came in the early afternoon and another chance had gone.

When Hutton arrived at The Oval with his Yorkshire colleagues it was for his sixth consecutive day of cricket and he found himself in the field. Yorkshire were bowling on a pitch that offered some help to the bowlers and with Bob Appleyard's three victims helping to reduce the home side to 105 for 5, the visitors were soon in the driving seat. Only Tom Clark made a score of any significance and when he had fallen to skipper Norman Yardley, Fred Trueman quickly disposed of the tail. The last five wickets fell for the addition of only 25 runs.

Len Hutton walks out to bat with opening partner Frank Lowson at Bournemouth in 1954. At The Oval in July 1951 the pair shared an opening stand of 197 as Hutton became the thirteenth batsman to reach the milestone of 100 first-class centuries.

Len Hutton leaving the field at The Oval after registering his 100th hundred and being applauded in by the Surrey players.

Yorkshire's reply began with Hutton and Frank Lowson making the game look much simpler than the Surrey batsman had done, and by close of play their stand had reached 112 with Hutton on 61. He then had Sunday on which to rest as well as prepare for what would be a huge amount of interest.

The 15,000 crowd who gave up their Monday morning (apparently a headmaster inspected the queue!) were full of eager anticipation. Hutton looked his normal unperturbed self and showed no anxiety in displaying his usual mannerism of regularly touching the peak of his cap. The spectators were not to be denied their historic moment, however, and in due course a cover-drive off Owen Wait sped to the boundary. The stroke was 'worthy of the occasion' being in Hutton's best mould and he had become the thirteenth batsman to score 100 centuries, in a grand manner. It had taken him 619 innings and only Don Bradman, at the time, had achieved it in fewer.

Now that, in some people's eyes, the main event of the day was fulfilled, Yorkshire continued on their way towards being in a winning position. It was not until a first-innings lead of 41 had been achieved that Surrey took their first wicket – that of Lowson. Hutton's partner was an accomplished opening batsman in his own right (he played in seven Tests for England) and on this occasion, as on many others, he displayed the same calm certainty and precision of timing as his more famous colleague. It was often said that it was difficult to distinguish between the two when watching from a distance.

Following a near-double century opening stand, Hutton was joined by Vic Wilson and the pair added a further 58 before Hutton passed 150 and was almost immediately bowled by Tony Lock. He had batted faultlessly for 280 minutes and had hit 12 fours. Although Jim Laker was proving difficult to score from, Wilson unleashed some fine drives and put on 129 for the third wicket with Geoffrey Keighley. Wilson was in a dominating mood and even Willie Watson scored only 16 of the unbroken stand of 47 for the fourth wicket before the declaration came. Wilson's century contained 3 sixes and 10 fours and was a

SURREY v. YORKSHIRE

major factor in Yorkshire gaining a big first-innings lead of 275. Incidentally, he and Keighley were the only members of the Yorkshire XI who played in this game who would never go on to represent England. This was despite Wilson being twelfth man in all of the Tests on the Ashes-winning tour of 1954/55.

Surrey now had an uphill struggle if they were to save the game. An early wicket was lost but more consistent contributions were now forthcoming. However, although the score almost reached 100 before the second wicket fell, three went down for the addition of only 14 runs. At 158 for 5, the home side was facing an innings defeat and still had a great deal to do. The determined Laurie Fishlock was then joined by wicketkeeper Arthur McIntyre and the pair put on 83 together in making Surrey's highest stand of the game. Meanwhile, Yorkshire were dropping vital catches but eventually the leg-spin of Eddie Leadbeater was responsible for the final two wickets. This was in his fiftieth over (he had not bowled in the first innings) and Surrey had been disposed of for a total that was more than double that of their first effort.

All of this left Yorkshire to score 43 runs in twenty minutes to gain victory. Unfortunately, the approach, including that of Hutton, was too frantic, smacking of panic, and they hit 'recklessly at every ball'. Alec Bedser was his usual metronomic self and he instigated a collapse in which four wickets fell for the addition of only three runs. The batsmen hurried between the pavilion gate and the crease but it was all to no avail as two more wickets were lost (both to run-outs) and Yorkshire ended 13 runs short. One cannot help but think that today's batsmen, brought up on a diet of limited-overs cricket, would have been equal to a task of scoring the 43 required in what became just six overs.

Nevertheless, the crowd had been royally entertained and it had been a fitting climax to an historic game.

Above left: Hutton is congratulated on his 100th hundred by Norman Yardley in The Oval dressing room. Looking on are Don Brennan (left) and Willie Watson (right).

Above right: How the newspapers recorded Hutton's 100th century.

SURREY v. YORKSHIRE

SURREY v. YORKSHIRE

Surrey won the toss and elected to bat

Umpires: H. Elliott and F.S. Lee

SURREY

Batsman	Dismissal (1st)	Runs	Dismissal (2nd)	Runs
M.R. Barton*	c Wilson b Yardley	14	b Wardle	39
E.A. Bedser	b Appleyard	22	c Brennan b Leadbeater	8
B. Constable	b Appleyard	16	c Wilson b Appleyard	47
L.B. Fishlock	lbw b Trueman	11	st Brennan b Wardle	89
J.F. Parker	b Appleyard	8	b Appleyard	4
T.H. Clark	c Brennan b Yardley	47	c Brennan b Trueman	15
A.J. McIntyre+	c Brennan b Wardle	8	b Leadbeater	32
J.C. Laker	c Wilson b Yardley	2	lbw b Wardle	13
A.V. Bedser	not out	11	not out	27
G.A.R. Lock	b Trueman	1	c Wilson b Leadbeater	23
O.J. Wait	b Trueman	4	c Wardle b Leadbeater	0
Extras	(b5 lb4 nb3)	12	(b8 lb4 w4 nb4)	20
TOTAL		156		317

FOW 1st: 19, 55, 67, 75, 105, 131, 136, 143, 144, 156
FOW 2nd: 10, 99, 107, 113, 158, 241, 259, 272, 315, 317

Bowling 1st: Trueman 19-2-52-3 Appleyard 21-8-53-3 Yardley 20-6-28-3 Wardle 9-3-11-1

Bowling 2nd: Trueman 22-7-26-4 Appleyard 23-5-54-2 Leadbeater 49.2-16-112-4 Hutton 3-0-12-0 Wardle 32-8-83-3 Yardley 3-0-10-0

YORKSHIRE

Batsman	Dismissal (1st)	Runs	Dismissal (2nd)	Runs
L. Hutton	b Lock	151	c Constable b Bedser	5
F.A. Lowson	c&b Parker	84	c Lock b Bedser	10
J.V. Wilson	not out	114	(4) not out	5
W.G. Keighley	b Wait	45	(6) run out	1
W. Watson	not out	16	run out	1
N.W.D. Yardley*			(3) c Fishlock b Wait	1
J.H. Wardle			b Wait	2
E. Leadbeater			not out	0
D.V. Brennan+				
R. Appleyard				
F.S. Trueman				
Extras	(b4 lb9 w4 nb4)	21	(lb4 nb1)	5
TOTAL	(3 wkts dec)	431	(6 wkts)	30

FOW 1st: 197, 255, 384
FOW 2nd: 19, 19, 20, 22, 27, 30

Bowling 1st: A. Bedser 38-5-106-0 Wait 19-2-65-1 Parker 15-4-38-1 Laker 35-10-71-0 Lock 22-6-58-1 E. Bedser 13-2-46-0 Clark 9-1-26-0

Bowling 2nd: A. Bedser 3-0-17-2 Wait 3-0-8-2

MATCH DRAWN

LANCASHIRE v. YORKSHIRE

Date: 2, 4, 5 August 1952   County Championship
Location: Old Trafford

Some of the most dramatic cricket matches end in stalemate. Such was the case in this classic Roses battle at Old Trafford in early August 1952 as Yorkshire chased Surrey for the Championship crown. Yorkshire would ultimately fall short as their southern rivals claimed top spot by a clear 32-point margin, which set off a winning sequence of seven successive County titles. Inconsistency was a feature of Lancashire's sea-

Sheffield-born bowler Eric Burgin captured five wickets in an innings in his first Roses match with his accurate in-swing.

son. They were beaten only three times (the same as eventual Champions Surrey), but drew 11 of their other games and managed just 12 outright victories compared with Surrey's 20 and Yorkshire's 17.

The first day's play (Saturday, 2 August) didn't get underway until 4.00p.m. due to rain and Len Hutton and Frank Lowson immediately dug in for the White Rose. A dour confrontation seemed most likely. However, that didn't prevent a typically large Roses crowd gathering on the Monday (20,000) and they were treated to a day's play that saw 23 wickets fall and 234 runs scored. The dying surface proved a formidable opponent for both sets of batsmen. Hutton top-scored for Yorkshire with 57, Lowson made 40 and Willie Watson fell one short of his 50. Fred Trueman had been granted leave by the RAF to play in the match. Indeed, he played in only nine first-class matches for Yorkshire that summer due to National Service and Test calls. He hit an unbeaten 23 as Lancashire's slow left-armed Bob Berry fully exploited the conditions to claim six wickets.

The Red Rose response was catastrophic. Against Trueman's pace and Eric Burgin's accurate in-swing, Lancashire registered their lowest innings total against Yorkshire at Old Trafford for forty-three years. The home side never recovered from being 15 for 4 and lost their last four wickets for only one run. Sheffield-born Burgin, in his first Roses' outing, had the marvellous figures of 5 for 20 and Trueman (who Burgin had coached at Sheffield United CC) claimed the rest as the visitors gained a 135-run first-innings lead. Yorkshire chased quick runs in their second innings finally declaring on the last day having set Lancashire 299 to win in three and three-quarter hours. Only Brian Close (61) made more than 20 in Yorkshire's second innings before the declaration came. Burgin was soon in the thick of things again, removing James Lomax for a duck; Lancashire 0 for 1. Jack Ikin and Geoff Edrich steadied the ship.

Indeed, for much of the remaining play, Lancashire, whilst never threatening to reach the required target, seemed equally

LANCASHIRE v. YORKSHIRE

unlikely to lose the game. However, that started to change as one by one wickets started to fall to poor and over-aggressive strokes. Johnny Wardle and Brian Close had removed the major part of Lancashire's batting, and as the last half-hour got underway, with Trueman and Burgin taking the new ball, the home side were deep in trouble at 157 for 7. Trueman bowled both Brian Statham and Roy Tattersall, and as last man Berry joined Frank Parr at the wicket, ten minutes of play remained. Despite Yorkshire's best efforts, the pair stayed together. Wicketkeeper Parr, having batted manfully for an hour, was nine not out when time ran out at 5.15p.m. More than 40,000 paying spectators over the three days had witnessed the game and Norman Yardley's men left Manchester ruing their missed opportunity despite having played out a gripping Roses contest.

LANCASHIRE v. YORKSHIRE

Yorkshire won the toss and elected to bat

Umpires: A.E. Pothecary and H. Elliott

YORKSHIRE

L. Hutton	c Lomax b Tattersall	57	lbw b Berry		16
F.A. Lowson	c&b Tattersall	40	c Parr b Statham		9
H. Halliday	c Grieves b Berry	2	b Tattersall		4
E.I. Lester	c Ikin b Berry	0	c Howard b Tattersall		20
W. Watson	c Grieves b Statham	49	c&b Tattersall		7
D.B. Close	c Grieves b Berry	2	c Berry b Tattersall		61
N.W.D. Yardley*	c Place b Berry	12	c Parr b Lomax		10
J.H. Wardle	c Howard b Tattersall	9	c Edrich b Lomax		4
D.V. Brennan+	lbw b Berry	1	not out		14
E. Burgin	c Parr b Berry	4	not out		2
F.S. Trueman	not out	23			
Extras	(w1)	1	(b8 lb3 w4 nb1)		16
TOTAL		200	(8 wkts dec)		163

FOW 1st: 98, 98, 99, 100, 106, 118, 131, 135, 145, 200
FOW 2nd: 23, 34, 36, 51, 88, 126, 132, 142

Bowling 1st: Statham 17.5-4-35-1 Lomax 20-6-29-0 Tattersall 26-7-77-3 Wharton 5-1-6-0 Berry 18-6-52-6

Bowling 2nd: Statham 17-3-53-1 Lomax 6-3-13-2 Tattersall 21-4-65-4 Berry 7-0-16-1

LANCASHIRE

J.T. Ikin	b Trueman	0	c Wardle b Close		41
J.G. Lomax	b Burgin	0	c Close b Burgin		0
G.A. Edrich	c Close b Burgin	4	c Halliday b Wardle		40
W. Place	c Brennan b Trueman	1	c Trueman b Close		11
K. Grieves	b Burgin	10	c Watson b Wardle		16
N.D. Howard*	c Hutton b Burgin	20	c Watson b Wardle		14
A. Wharton	c Watson b Burgin	14	lbw b Halliday		15
F.D. Parr+	b Trueman	5	not out		9
J.B. Statham	b Trueman	0	b Trueman		0
R. Tattersall	lbw b Trueman	0	b Trueman		0
R. Berry	not out	0	not out		1
Extras	(b8 nb3)	11	(b12 lb4 nb3)		19
TOTAL		65	(9 wkts)		166

FOW 1st: 4, 9, 13, 15, 45, 46, 64, 64, 64, 65
FOW 2nd: 0, 69, 94, 99, 131, 131, 157, 157,165

Bowling 1st: Trueman 10.2-5-26-5 Burgin 12-3-20-5 Wardle 2-1-8-0

Bowling 2nd: Trueman 20-6-42-2 Burgin 11-3-24-1 Wardle 27-13-57-3 Close 8-3-17-2 Halliday 8-6-7-1

MATCH DRAWN

YORKSHIRE v. LEICESTERSHIRE

Date: 16, 17, 18 June 1954   County Championship
Location: Huddersfield

This was a game in which the two sides matched each other so well, on an innings-by-innings basis, that the eventual result was as close as it is possible to be. Yorkshire came into the game unbeaten, having won six and drawn the remaining four of their first ten games. Surrey had won both of the previous two Championship titles and the White Rose county were chasing them hard as they attempted a hat-trick. Leicestershire, in the meantime, were experiencing a poor season and were not expected to put up much in the way of opposition.

The first innings of the game went very much to form as Yorkshire compiled a score in excess of 350 and declared with only four wickets down. The stars of this particular show were two left-handers – Vic Wilson and Willie Watson – who mounted a punishing fourth-wicket partnership of 168 that lasted less than two hours.

Leicestershire's reply showed that they were no pushovers and they did not lose their second wicket until the score had reached 183. In fact, they batted so well that by the time they were only 36 runs behind they still had five wickets left. Most of the credit for this was due to Maurice Tompkin who held the innings together after Gerry Lester, opening the batting at the age of thirty-eight, had contributed a solid half-century. After Tompkin had been dismissed, stumped one run short of 150, the innings quickly folded, the last five wickets falling for a paltry 13 runs and the home side had a narrow lead of 23. Johnny Wardle had been the pick of the bowlers in conceding fewer than two runs per over and taking four wickets.

The weather changed quickly at this point and increasing cloud cover started to encourage swing bowling. So difficult did this make batting, in comparison with the previous part of the game, that Yorkshire soon found themselves to be 43 for 4 and Terry Spencer had taken all of the wickets to fall. Although Ted Lester and Norman Yardley added 39 together for the fifth wicket, another collapse ensued, and so well did Spencer exploit the conditions that he took nine wickets and his team would require only 136 to win.

Anything that Spencer could do, Fred Trueman could do better – to begin with, anyway. The visitors made an even worse start and collapsed to 29 for 5, four of these to Trueman. Charles Palmer and Vic Munden mounted a rescue act and Jack Walsh also helped the score to reach a situation whereby Leicestershire needed 14 to win with four wickets left. Time was a factor also, as the extra half-hour had already been claimed. There should not have been any need to panic, but Palmer got himself run out, Walsh was caught, and then Jack Firth stepped out of his crease only to be stumped. All of this left the last pair to score ten for victory.

Johnny Wardle was involved in the last three wickets, including – off the last ball of the match – the run out of Spencer to tie the game.

YORKSHIRE v. LEICESTERSHIRE

No.11, Brian Boshier, was one of the worst batsmen in history and was suffering from sciatica, not having bowled in Yorkshire's second innings. So it was down to Spencer to be a hero again. He gradually inched towards the target and, with the very last ball to be bowled by Wardle, the scores were level. Spencer played the ball down the pitch and set off for the winning run. Wardle quickly gathered the ball, threw down the wicket and, with Spencer not having made his ground, the match was tied.

It was the first tied match in Yorkshire's history and there has been only one other since (see page 98).

YORKSHIRE v. LEICESTERSHIRE

Yorkshire won the toss and elected to bat

Umpires: E. Cooke and H. Elliott

YORKSHIRE

L. Hutton	c Firth b Munden	60	c Firth b Spencer	6
F.A. Lowson	b Walsh	38	b Spencer	8
J.V. Wilson	c Palmer b Walsh	138	b Spencer	18
E.I. Lester	c Boshier b Palmer	33	b Spencer	34
W. Watson	not out	80	b Spencer	0
N.W.D. Yardley*			b Spencer	22
D.B. Close			c Firth b Palmer	1
J.H. Wardle			b Spencer	0
R. Booth+			c Smithson b Spencer	8
R. Appleyard			not out	1
F.S. Trueman			b Spencer	8
Extras	(lb1 nb1)	2	(b4 lb1 nb2)	7
TOTAL	(4 wkts dec)	351		113

FOW 1st: 82, 123, 183, 351
FOW 2nd: 13, 18, 43, 43, 82, 85, 87, 97, 108, 113

Bowling 1st: Spencer 25-3-70-0 Boshier 17-3-51-0 Palmer 12-4-33-1 Walsh 20.5-0-77-2
Jackson 14-3-52-0 Munden 23-4-66-1

Bowling 2nd: Spencer 23-3-63-9 Palmer 12-6-18-1 Jackson 10-2-25-0

LEICESTERSHIRE

G. Lester	b Close	74	b Trueman	4
M.R. Hallam	b Trueman	24	b Trueman	2
M. Tompkin	st Booth b Wardle	149	c&b Appleyard	6
C.H. Palmer*	c Hutton b Wardle	15	(5) b Wardle	31
V.E. Jackson	c Booth b Trueman	1	(6) c Lester b Trueman	4
G.A. Smithson	c&b Close	25	(4) c Lowson b Trueman	0
V.S. Munden	b Appleyard	19	run out	31
J.E. Walsh	b Wardle	0	c Hutton b Wardle	28
J. Firth+	not out	8	(10) st Booth b Wardle	3
C.T. Spencer	st Booth b Appleyard	0	(9) run out	8
B.S. Boshier	c Watson b Wardle	1	not out	1
Extras	(b8 lb4)	12	(b6 lb11 nb1)	18
TOTAL		328		136

FOW 1st: 58, 183, 216, 223, 281, 315, 315, 327, 327, 328
FOW 2nd: 8, 15, 19, 21, 29, 72, 123, 123, 127, 136

Bowling 1st: Trueman 22-1-83-2 Appleyard 31-11-62-2 Yardley 6-1-22-0 Wardle 44.4-18-82-4
Close 21-3-67-2

Bowling 2nd: Trueman 18-2-44-4 Appleyard 20-8-38-1 Wardle 13-4-36-3

MATCH TIED

WORCESTERSHIRE v. YORKSHIRE

Date: 27, 29, 30 July 1957

County Championship

Location: Worcester

Although this game's second innings had not been completed when the final day began, Yorkshire gained a pulsating victory that was inspired by the extremely accurate bowling of a certain off-spinner named Raymond Illingworth.

Yorkshire went into this match pushing strongly for the runners-up spot in the Championship. Surrey had won five titles in a row and were already so far ahead that second place was all that was realistically left to play for. Worcestershire, in complete contrast, were having a poor season and were in serious danger of finishing bottom for the first time since 1932.

The home side looked comfortable enough to start with, however, and without Fred Trueman on Test duty the visitors' attack lacked its usual cutting edge. Worcestershire's openers put on 72 before both were dismissed by Illingworth, Don Kenyon just failing to reach a half-century. Wickets fell intermittently thereafter as Worcestershire failed to capitalise on their good start. Four bowlers shared the wickets with Illingworth producing the best figures and Johnny Wardle (conceding only 34 runs from 24 overs) being the most economical.

Six of Worcestershire's batsmen had passed 20 but none had gone on to produce a significant score. When the White Rose county had reached 133 for 4 with each batsman getting out for scores of between 21 and 38, it seemed that their innings might follow suit. Willie Watson then changed the game's course with a solid display that lasted three and a half hours. His score of 80 was the highest of the match and his stand of 90 for the fifth wicket with Illingworth took Yorkshire to within 14 runs of the Midland county's total. Billy Sutcliffe, in his second season as captain, then shared 68 runs with Watson and the second day ended with the score on 293 for 7. On the final morning the tail contributed well and Yorkshire gained a first-innings lead of 106 runs but it seemed unlikely that there would be time for them to achieve victory.

This view was reinforced when Worcestershire's openers produced another half-century stand and, with the pitch being very easy-paced, there seemed to be no need for alarm. Once Illingworth had found a certain spot that produced enough turn and bounce, however, the progress of the match was completely transformed. He and Wardle bowled 63 of the 76 overs that the visitors sent down in this pivotal innings of the game and Illingworth captured figures that he never bettered in his entire first-class career. His nine wickets contrasted starkly with Wardle's single success but the latter made sure that the batsmen gained no respite from the pressure as the game swung decisively Yorkshire's way.

Len Outschoorn defied the attack for a gallant half-century but with all 10 wickets tumbling for only 115 runs the visitors were left an hour in which to score 67 to gain a victory that had looked only a distant possibility just a few hours earlier. It was certainly not plain sailing and Yorkshire's scorecard soon showed 18 for 3. The final

Willie Watson – top scorer in Yorkshire's first innings.

WORCESTERSHIRE v. YORKSHIRE

decisive performance came from the batting of Brian Close whose telling blows in an unbeaten innings of 41, with Watson playing another sheet anchor role, saw Yorkshire home with just five minutes to spare.

Yorkshire lost only one of their remaining eight games but had to be content with third place. Despite being 28 points adrift of Northamptonshire, it was a further 94 points between them and Surrey's final total. Illingworth would go on to take 100 wickets for the second season in succession and would make his Test debut in less than twelve months' time. But he would never again take nine wickets in an innings.

WORCESTERSHIRE v. YORKSHIRE

Worcestershire won the toss and elected to bat

Umpires: P.A. Gibb and T.J. Bartley

WORCESTERSHIRE

D. Kenyon	b Illingworth	47	b Illingworth	28
L. Outschoorn	b Illingworth	32	lbw b Illingworth	60
G. Dews	c Taylor b Appleyard	21	lbw b Illingworth	6
D.W. Richardson	st Binks b Wardle	20	st Binks b Wardle	13
R.G. Broadbent	b Pickles	14	c Stott b Illingworth	16
M.J. Horton	c Binks b Wardle	38	c Close b Illingworth	12
R. Booth+	st Binks b Appleyard	2	b Illingworth	11
R.O. Jenkins*	b Appleyard	26	not out	7
R. Berry	b Illingworth	12	c Wilson b Illingworth	8
J.A. Flavell	c&b Pickles	3	st Binks b Illingworth	0
L.J. Coldwell	not out	0	c Stott b Illingworth	1
Extras	(b9 lb6 nb7)	22	(b9 lb1)	10
TOTAL		237		172

FOW 1st: 72, 85, 128, 128, 172, 179, 189, 206, 217, 237
FOW 2nd: 57, 71, 107, 127, 132, 147, 154, 168, 168, 172

Bowling 1st: Pickles 14-2-35-2 Appleyard 23-5-63-3 Illingworth 23-10-49-3 Close 10-1-34-0 Wardle 24-14-34-2

Bowling 2nd: Pickles 4-0-25-0 Appleyard 3-0-18-0 Illingworth 32-15-42-9 Wardle 31-16-51-1 Close 6-2-26-0

YORKSHIRE

W.B. Stott	c Jenkins b Flavell	21	b Berry	5
K. Taylor	c Coldwell b Berry	27	lbw b Berry	8
J.V. Wilson	c Booth b Horton	38	c Jenkins b Coldwell	1
D.B. Close	b Jenkins	38	not out	41
W. Watson	c&b Jenkins	80	not out	9
R. Illingworth	c Broadbent b Richardson	58		
W.H.H. Sutcliffe*	lbw b Berry	27		
J.H. Wardle	b Coldwell	1		
J.G. Binks+	st Booth b Jenkins	19		
R. Appleyard	c Berry b Jenkins	23		
D. Pickles	not out	0		
Extras	(b2 lb4 w4 nb1)	11	(lb3 nb1)	4
TOTAL		343	(3 wkts)	68

FOW 1st: 25, 78, 91, 133, 223, 291, 292, 317, 330, 343
FOW 2nd: 13, 14, 18

Bowling 1st: Flavell 11-3-31-1 Coldwell 27-7-73-1 Berry 23-3-73-2 Horton 23-12-57-1 Jenkins 16.4-3-68-4 Richardson 8-1-30-1

Bowling 2nd: Coldwell 8-1-21-1 Berry 7.5-0-43-2

YORKSHIRE WON BY SEVEN WICKETS

SUSSEX v. YORKSHIRE

Date: 29, 31 August, 1 September 1959   County Championship
Location: Hove

The English season of 1959 will be remembered both for the glorious weather that accompanied much of the cricket played and, in county circles, the end of Surrey's seven-year reign as title holders. After three previously wet summers, county cricket attendances were up by 40% in 1959. Followers of the game revelled in a thrilling finish to the Championship campaign that finally brought Yorkshire their first outright title for thirteen years, thus ending their longest barren sequence in the Club's history to that point since the formation of the official County Championship competition in 1890. The issue was not decided until the first day of September when Ronnie Burnet's young side completed their stirring run-chase over Sussex at Hove.

Yorkshire's challenge for their twenty-third county crown (since 1890) had faltered badly in their final three games prior to the encounter with Sussex. Defeats were sustained against Somerset at Bath (just 16 runs) and then against fellow Championship contenders Gloucestershire, by an innings and 77 runs, at Bristol. Victory in a run chase against the clock over Worcestershire by six wickets in their penultimate game revived White Rose hopes. Yet Burnet's chargers still faced a 'must-win' situation at Hove.

Sussex, led by Robin Marlar (in his last season as skipper), batted first on the opening morning and were in some difficulty at 67 for 6. Ken Taylor, operating as first change bowler, enjoyed a successful spell for the visitors, taking four of the first five wickets that went down. Don Smith and 'Tiger' Pataudi steadied the decline by adding 90 for the seventh wicket. Smith fell one short of his 50 and Pataudi was bowled by Fred Trueman for 52, but the pair helped Sussex to a respectable 210 all out after their early-innings col-

Bryan Stott (left) and Doug Padgett shared a third-wicket stand of 141 in sixty-one minutes in Yorkshire's epic second-innings charge to victory and the Championship title.

lapse. Yorkshire's innings initially followed a similar pattern. Ted Dexter, with his medium-pace bowling, removed Brian Bolus, Doug Padgett and Brian Close cheaply before Bryan Stott and Ray Illingworth came together. Stott was caught and bowled by Ken Suttle, having added 40 with Illingworth. Taylor's dismissal for three left Yorkshire 81 for 5. Aided by firstly Jack Birkenshaw (38) and then Don Wilson, with a hard-hitting half-century, Illingworth batted with great maturity in making 122 (his second Championship hundred of the season) in just under five hours, with 17 fours. Sussex, having cleared the first-innings deficit of 97 for the loss of only two wickets (Alan Oakman and Suttle), batted with far greater cohesion and took the game into the last day with the Championship title hinging on the result.

Play on that final day was scheduled to end at 4.30p.m., which also included the extra half-hour if required. The Sussex skipper made it clear to Yorkshire that he had no intention of declaring with the Championship at stake and batted on throughout the morning session and after lunch. Jim Parks batted

Ray Illingworth and Brian Bolus return to the pavilion having completed Yorkshire's victory chase.

with purpose, top-scoring with 85. With Trueman a spent force, Burnet relied on his spinners Wilson and Illingworth to close down the Sussex resistance. The last three Sussex wickets fell to Illingworth. Birkenshaw took four excellent catches on the square leg boundary, including Marlar's first ball. Yorkshire's final task seemed an improbable one – 215 runs to win in only 105 available minutes at the crease.

In the dressing room, the decision was made to go for the target. The batting order was altered: Stott and Close opened; Taylor was listed as no.3 with Padgett at no.4. Yorkshire's intentions were made clear from the start. Stott hit 13 of the 15 scored from the first over to set the tone for what followed. Close made a quick dozen before being caught behind. The six he struck over the scoreboard cost his side a few vital moments (three precious minutes in fact!) whilst the ball was recovered. Taylor went quickly but the pace of the innings didn't falter. The 50 was registered in only twenty minutes as Padgett now joined Stott and the bold assault gathered even greater momentum. The Sussex tactics were quickly in turmoil. Marlar started with a normal field but after a couple of overs he realised that Yorkshire had no intentions of playing defensively and at various stages thereafter as many as seven men were posted around the boundary. Stott and Padgett ran brilliantly between the wickets, turning singles into twos at every opportunity to counter the Sussex ploy of defensive fields and in between maintained the run-rate with some thrilling stroke-play. The score had reached 77 after only thirty minutes of the Yorkshire innings. The 100 took forty-three minutes, the next 50 a mere twenty minutes and 200 was on the board after less than one and a half hours of quite sensational batting. Padgett and Stott scored 141 together in sixty-one minutes.

SUSSEX v. YORKSHIRE

By the time Padgett was caught at deep mid-wicket by Dexter off Ian Thomson, Yorkshire needed only 34 more runs for victory. Stott batted only eighty-six minutes for his 96. It was left to Bolus, with a glance to the fine leg boundary, to seal Yorkshire's unlikely conquest at Hove at 4.23p.m. With Surrey only able to hang on for a draw against Middlesex at The Oval, the Championship title was Yorkshire's. The new County Champions had reached their objective with seven minutes to spare in a mere 28.3 overs, and as Jim Kilburn wrote in the following day's *Yorkshire Post,* 'It was victory against expectation, against probability, against reason...' The enthusiastic Hove crowd swarmed onto the County Ground to hail an exhibition of truly belligerent cricket that had finally wrestled the Championship pennant from the seven-year grip of Surrey CCC.

A joyous Scarborough crowd welcomed Yorkshire's victorious side the following day for their match against the MCC. The style and manner of Yorkshire's play at Hove continued with yet another fine run-chase. Set 260 in two and a half hours, they got home with twenty-five minutes to spare, and in mid-September beat The Rest of England in the traditional fixture against the Champion County at The Oval by 66 runs. Burnet's two-year tenure as captain finished there. Yorkshire's new-found spirit, which carried them to success and glory in the 1960s, had been forged during his reign and was sealed with the side's breathtaking victory at Hove on 1 September 1959.

Above: The Yorkshire players and staff celebrate the Championship title and their victory at Hove.

Left: Yorkshire's skipper Ronnie Burnet.

SUSSEX v. YORKSHIRE

SUSSEX v. YORKSHIRE

Sussex won the toss and elected to bat

Umpires: R.S. Lay and F.S. Lee

SUSSEX

A.S.M. Oakman	st Binks b Taylor	33	b Close	7
L.J. Lenham	c Taylor b Trueman	4	c Stott b Wilson	66
K.G. Suttle	c Illingworth b Taylor	5	st Binks b Wilson	22
E.R. Dexter	c&b Taylor	14	c Birkenshaw b Wilson	33
J.M. Parks+	c Bolus b Taylor	6	c Birkenshaw b Wilson	85
G.H.G. Doggart	lbw b Close	5	c Birkenshaw b Illingworth	10
D.V. Smith	c Close b Illingworth	49	c Bolus b Taylor	31
Nawab of Pataudi	b Trueman	52	c Close b Illingworth	37
N.I. Thomson	lbw b Illingworth	21	b Illingworth	12
A.E. James	b Illingworth	4	not out	0
R.G. Marlar*	not out	13	c Birkenshaw b Illingworth	0
Extras	(lb4)	4	(b4 lb4)	8
TOTAL		210		311

FOW 1st: 28, 40, 51, 62, 63, 67, 157, 192, 193, 210
FOW 2nd: 14, 80, 99, 174, 195, 247, 266, 306, 311, 311

Bowling 1st: Trueman 19-5-40-2 Close 17-5-54-1 Taylor 22-9-40-4 Illingworth 14.2-3-51-3 Wilson 5-1-21-0

Bowling 2nd: Trueman 24-5-60-0 Close 19-6-51-1 Illingworth 28.3-8-66-4 Taylor 8-5-5-1 Birkenshaw 7-0-43-0
Wilson 24-7-78-4

YORKSHIRE

W.B. Stott	c&b Suttle	34	(1) c N of Pataudi b Marlar	96
B. Bolus	hit wkt b Dexter	1	(7) not out	6
D.E.V. Padgett	c Parks b Dexter	0	(4) b Thomson	79
D.B. Close	b Dexter	14	(3) c Parks b Dexter	12
R. Illingworth	c Parks b James	122	(6) not out	5
K. Taylor	lbw b Thomson	3	(2) lbw b Dexter	1
J. Birkenshaw	lbw b Marlar	38		
D. Wilson	c Oakman b Marlar	55		
J.R. Burnet*	c Marlar b Dexter	1		
F.S. Trueman	c N of Pataudi b James	7	(4) st Parks b Marlar	11
J.G. Binks+	not out	1		
Extras	(b24 lb6 nb1)	31	(b1 lb4 nb3)	8
TOTAL		307	(5 wkts)	218

FOW 1st: 6, 6, 38, 78, 81, 193, 259, 264, 305, 307
FOW 2nd: 18, 40, 181, 199, 206

Bowling 1st: Thomson 31-7-65-1 Dexter 29-7-63-4 Smith 4-1-14-0 James 24-4-67-2 Marlar 15.4-7-29-2
Suttle 6-1-20-1 Oakman 6-1-18-0 Doggart 1-1-0-0

Bowling 2nd: Thomson 10-0-87-1 Dexter 10.3-0-69-2 James 2-0-15-0 Marlar 6-0-39-2

YORKSHIRE WON BY FIVE WICKETS

YORKSHIRE v. THE REST OF ENGLAND

Date: 12, 14, 15 September 1959   First-class friendly challenge match
Location: The Oval

Having won the Championship in such fine style, the Yorkshire team might have expected some respite from their labours. There was to be no such luck, however, and, following a long drive from Hove to Scarborough, ten of the victorious eleven were in action again the following morning as the Festival began with a game against the MCC – the host county's thirty-fifth game of the season.

Four of these ten were involved in other Festival games before they all made the final journey to The Oval and the season's last challenge. And what a challenge! All other first-class cricket had now finished so the selectors had the opportunity to put out a very strong side, players from all of the other sixteen counties being available. Of the eleven chosen, only one, Bob Gale, would never be a Test player.

Gale, however, took the eye with immediate effect, helping produce a century opening stand for The Rest. His partner, Geoff Pullar, scored a century before lunch, 70 of his runs coming in boundaries. Others cashed in on the tired attack with Mike Smith and Trevor Bailey scoring half-centuries. The former had already become the first batsman to score 3,000 runs in a season for ten years, and Bailey completed the first 2,000-run and 100-wicket 'double' since 1937. Yorkshire's spinners suffered most with Brian Close conceding runs at a rate of more than six an over. Illingworth was suffering from a worn spinning finger.

The Champions' reply could not have been more contrasting. Brian Bolus was bowled on the first evening and the scoreboard soon read 16 for 4 on day two thanks to Harold Rhodes and Alan Moss. Although Close led a rally that was continued by Vic Wilson and Illingworth, The Rest's spinners also cashed in, Ken Barrington taking all of the last three wickets. The Rest had a massive first-innings lead of 224 and Yorkshire, their collective tail between their legs, were duly asked to follow on.

The northern county's response was now far more positive; there was an opening stand of 78 but the game's real turning point was a fourth-wicket partnership of 124 between Close and Wilson. The latter had not played for the county for over a month and had gone into this game with only 462 runs at an average of less than 20 and no hundreds to show for a season's work. Indeed, his selection for this game had only

Brian Close – 5 for 47 in The Rest of England's second innings and 86 in Yorkshire's second innings having followed-on.

narrowly been achieved. He batted for over four hours and, although Barrington again took two quick wickets, Illingworth, Trueman and Jimmy Binks were all able to make telling contributions and take the total to over 400 and secure the county's highest total for the whole season.

The Rest thus faced a victory target of 202 but made the mistake of juggling their batting order. Although a good start was made, once Bob Platt had effected the initial breakthrough all 10 wickets fell for only 94 runs, the rest of the wickets falling to Illingworth and Close. It took

YORKSHIRE v. THE REST OF ENGLAND

only 41.4 overs and the match finished at precisely 6.00p.m. in a comfortable victory for the Champions. It was only the second time that Yorkshire had won a game after following on (see page 62), since the relevant law had changed in the previous century.

Not only did Vic Wilson's century change the outcome of this match, it probably changed the course of his career. Aged thirty-eight, he could well have not been offered a contract. Instead, Ronnie Burnet was asked to resign and Wilson became Yorkshire's first professional captain for almost eighty years.

YORKSHIRE v. THE REST OF ENGLAND

The Rest won the toss and elected to bat

Umpires: J.F. Crapp and H. Elliott

THE REST OF ENGLAND

G. Pullar	b Trueman	103	(3) c Stott b Close		4
R.A. Gale	c&b D. Wilson	40	(1) c Padgett b Platt		11
K.F. Barrington	st Binks b Illingworth	15	(4) c Bolus b Illingworth		18
M.J.K. Smith	c Padgett b Illingworth	77	(5) c Padgett b Close		25
D.B. Carr*	c Close b Platt	13	(6) c J.V Wilson b Illingworth		7
T.E. Bailey	c&b D. Wilson	59	(2) st Binks b Illingworth		32
T.G. Evans+	c Close b Platt	10	c Trueman b Close		27
D.A. Allen	b Close	6	(9) c Illingworth b Close		2
G.A.R. Lock	not out	44	(8) c Padgett b Illingworth		2
H.J. Rhodes	not out	10	not out		0
A.E. Moss			c J.V Wilson b Close		7
Extras	(lb7)	7	(b2 lb5)		7
TOTAL	(8 wkts dec)	384			135

FOW 1st: 138, 146, 196, 249, 250, 264, 288, 359
FOW 2nd: 41, 49, 53, 96, 96, 120, 132, 134, 135, 135

Bowling 1st: Trueman 27-8-61-1 Platt 17-6-40-2 Illingworth 28-4-109-2 Close 15-1-92-1
D. Wilson 16-3-75-2

Bowling 2nd: Trueman 8-2-18-0 Platt 8-2-23-1 Illingworth 13-2-40-4 Close 12.4-1-47-5

YORKSHIRE

W.B. Stott	b Moss	5	c Lock b Rhodes		61
J.B. Bolus	b Moss	1	lbw b Lock		44
J.G. Binks+	c Smith b Rhodes	3	(10) not out		21
D.E.V. Padgett	b Rhodes	2	(3) c Lock b Allen		18
D.B. Close	c Bailey b Lock	34	(4) b Bailey		86
J.V. Wilson	b Allen	41	(5) c Pullar b Allen		105
R. Illingworth	c Carr b Barrington	37	(6) hit wkt b Allen		32
D. Wilson	c Gale b Lock	9	(7) b Barrington		0
J.R. Burnet*	not out	17	(8) b Barrington		0
F.S. Trueman	b Barrington	5	(9) c Gale b Lock		45
R.K. Platt	b Barrington	4	b Lock		3
Extras	(lb2)	2	(b4 lb5 nb1)		10
TOTAL		160			425

FOW 1st: 2, 9, 9, 16, 70, 96, 111, 142, 150, 160
FOW 2nd: 78, 131, 132, 256, 318, 319, 323, 382, 410, 425

Bowling 1st: Rhodes 8-2-31-2 Moss 6-2-16-2 Lock 12-3-36-2 Bailey 6-1-22-0 Allen 8-1-35-1
Barrington 5-0-18-3

Bowling 2nd: Rhodes 15-4-66-1 Moss 13-1-46-0 Bailey 12-1-31-1 Lock 27.5-7-107-3 Allen 24-6-85-3 Barrington 22-4-72-2 Carr 2-0-8-0

YORKSHIRE WON BY 66 RUNS

WORCESTERSHIRE v. YORKSHIRE

Date: 3, 5, 6 June 1961   County Championship
Location: Worcester

Yorkshire came to Worcester as County Champions, having won the trophy in each of the previous two seasons. They were again expected to do well and had already won five of their first six matches. Worcestershire, however, had never won the title but were in the process of building a strong side that would finish in the top five in six of the next seven seasons, including their first two table-topping successes. These ingredients, plus the twists and turns of the first two days of this game, made for a fascinating contest that reached a gripping climax at the end of the final day.

Worcestershire's top order batted consistently in the first innings but only Ron Headley passed the half-century mark. The off-spin of Ray Illingworth induced a middle-order collapse and the last six wickets fell for only 35 runs with none of the last six batsmen getting into double figures. The last three wickets were all taken by Brian Close who had been pressed into service because of an injury to Don Wilson. The left-arm spinner had earlier made an attempt at a caught-and-bowled dismissal from Dick Richardson and had fractured his left thumb in the process, having bowled only two overs.

Yorkshire's reply to the all-out score of 227 began with a century stand from the two Brians – Stott and Bolus – but was also followed by an off-spin-led collapse as five wickets fell for 36 runs. The successful bowler was Martin Horton but skipper Vic Wilson, who put on 50 for the sixth wicket with Fred Trueman, came to the rescue. Trueman hit 8 fours before Alf Bainbridge, on his first-class debut, also chipped in usefully and Wilson was able to declare with a 38-run lead.

Headley again top-scored for Worcestershire in an innings total that produced exactly the same score as on the first attempt. Again there was a middle-order collapse as 166 for 4 became 174 for 8. Yorkshire-born Roy Booth helped Headley in the resistance but Trueman, with four wickets, was the most successful bowler. With Illingworth not being fit enough to bowl, Bainbridge showed promise by taking three wickets at important times in an economical spell.

Batting with his arm in plaster from the elbow to the knuckles (fractured thumb), Don Wilson scored an unbeaten 29 (mostly with one hand) to help Yorkshire to victory by one wicket.

Yorkshire's target was therefore 190 and they made a dreadful start by being reduced to 86 for 7 – the most ignominious of the game's four collapses – three wickets falling to the pace of Jack Flavell. The injured Illingworth and Jimmy Binks added 60 for the eighth wicket in only fifty-five minutes but when both fell within eight runs of each other the target became 36 with the last pair at the wicket.

The last two batsmen were Bob Platt (current career average 6.71) and Don Wilson with a left forearm encased in plaster. No less than twenty-five minutes remained for Yorkshire to save the game. Wilson soon realised that batting two-handed was too painful and winced with every contact. He managed to sweep fellow left-arm spinner

WORCESTERSHIRE v. YORKSHIRE

Norman Gifford for two fours but with only five minutes remaining and 22 runs still required for victory the final twist came. Don Kenyon, who himself had been for an X-ray having been struck on the left wrist by a ball from Trueman, gave the new ball to Flavell. Wilson's response was to drive him for three boundaries and a present of four byes meant that only four were required from the final over.

Platt nudged Len Coldwell for a single and, amid considerable excitement, Wilson struck the fourth ball for a lofted straight drive and the celebrations began. A match that was supposed to end in grim survival had ended in spectacular victory.

WORCESTERSHIRE v. YORKSHIRE

Worcestershire won the toss and elected to bat

Umpires: T.W. Spencer and F. Jakeman

WORCESTERSHIRE

D. Kenyon*	c J.V. Wilson b Trueman	30	c J.V. Wilson b Bainbridge		34
M.J. Horton	b Platt	13	c Binks b Trueman		6
R.G.A. Headley	st Binks b Close	61	c Binks b Trueman		49
D.W. Richardson	c Close b Illingworth	23	c sub b Close		5
G. Dews	c Stott b Illingworth	47	b Bainbridge		14
R.G. Broadbent	b Illingworth	5	(8) b Trueman		4
R. Booth+	lbw b Illingworth	6	(6) run out		31
J.A. Standen	b Close	0	(7) b Bainbridge		23
N. Gifford	not out	6	not out		12
L.J. Coldwell	c&b Close	4	b Trueman		25
J.A. Flavell	c J.V. Wilson b Close	2	c Padgett b Platt		11
Extras	(b14 lb8 w5 nb3)	30	(b11 lb1 nb1)		13
TOTAL		227			227

FOW 1st: 44, 48, 106, 165, 192, 209, 211, 211, 219, 227
FOW 2nd: 19, 58, 109, 123, 166, 166, 173, 174, 205, 227

Bowling 1st: Trueman 14-4-33-1 Platt 15-5-43-1 Illingworth 29-13-47-4 D. Wilson 2-1-13-0
Bainbridge 18-8-34-0 Close 9.1-3-27-4

Bowling 2nd: Trueman 27-9-50-4 Platt 17.3-6-43-1 Close 14-4-69-1 Bainbridge 31-16-52-3

YORKSHIRE

W.B. Stott	c Dews b Horton	46	c Standen b Flavell	5
J.B. Bolus	c Stranden b Gifford	54	b Coldwell	5
D.E.V. Padgett	c Booth b Horton	6	c sub b Flavell	7
D.B. Close	c sub b Horton	11	c sub b Flavell	15
R. Illingworth	c Headley b Horton	5	lbw b Coldwell	42
J.V. Wilson*	run out	49	lbw b Horton	16
F.S. Trueman	b Coldwell	43	c Flavell b Gifford	7
A.B. Bainbridge	c Standen b Horton	24	b Horton	0
J.G. Binks+	c Richardson b Flavell	19	b Flavell	46
R.K. Platt	not out	0	not out	7
D. Wilson			not out	29
Extras	(b4 lb4)	8	(b8 lb4)	12
TOTAL	(9 wkts dec)	265	(9 wkts)	191

FOW 1st: 100, 108, 119, 119, 136, 186, 224, 257, 265
FOW 2nd: 6, 14, 32, 36, 75, 86, 86, 146, 154

Bowling 1st: Flavell 16-4-38-1 Coldwell 10-4-22-1 Gifford 40-18-74-1 Horton 44-18-110-5
Standen 5-1-13-0

Bowling 2nd: Flavell 24-10-45-4 Coldwell 10.4-7-17-2 Gifford 34-15-80-1 Horton 19-7-37-2

YORKSHIRE WON BY ONE WICKET

YORKSHIRE v. HAMPSHIRE

Date: 27, 28, 29 June 1962   County Championship
Location: Bradford

Hampshire, under the inspired leadership of Colin Ingleby-Mackenzie, had claimed their first Championship crown in 1961 at the expense of Vic Wilson's Yorkshire side, who had had to settle for the runners-up spot after two successive titles in 1959 and 1960. Apart from Ingleby-Mackenzie's enthusiastic captaincy, Hampshire's success stemmed from the batting of Jimmy Gray, Henry Horton and the West Indian Roy Marshall, the all-round play of Peter Sainsbury and the craft and bowling skill of Derek Shackleton.

The meeting between the two sides at Bradford witnessed fluctuating changes of fortune to the very last delivery and culminated in a thrilling finish. On a lively first-day pitch and on a cool and cloudy morning, Shackleton was more than a handful for the Yorkshire batsmen. He bowled throughout the innings (three hours and forty minutes) and in his 31 overs the veteran seamer, mixing his usual tonic of control and swing both ways, claimed seven scalps. At lunch, Yorkshire were 71 for 5. The Yorkshire skipper Vic Wilson made a hard-fought 51 that lifted his side's total just over the 150 mark. Without opener Marshall, who was suffering with German measles, Hampshire appeared well placed at 102 for 1 with Mike Barnard and Henry Horton at the wicket. The removal of both – by Fred Trueman – was the start of a steady loss of wickets in mid-innings on day two before a real tumble at the end.

Hampshire lost their fifth wicket at 145 and their tenth at 165 to give them a slender lead of 14. Trueman (the Club's worthy beneficiary that season), in his usual style, removed nine and ten in the batting order and registered yet another five-wicket haul. Fast bowler David 'Butch' White and Shackleton (once again) were the major second-innings wicket-takers for Hampshire. White had Brian Bolus caught at the wicket without scoring, bowled Bryan Stott for 21 and sent back Ray Illingworth for 13. Shackleton chipped in with the wickets of Phil Sharpe and Doug Padgett as the home side at 70 for 6 appeared destined for defeat against the reigning Champions. However, Wilson 'again fought gamely,' and with support from Trueman virtually doubled Yorkshire's total. Top scorer once more with 45, Wilson finally succumbed to Shackleton who finished the innings with 5 for 67 and match figures of 12 for 145.

Hampshire required 163 for victory. Mike Cowan made the first breakthrough for Yorkshire having Horton caught behind by Jimmy Binks for 12. But although wickets fell at 41 and 97, Hampshire seemed well on course to their target with opener Gray steadfast (his 78 was made in four hours at the crease). He and Danny Livingstone raised the total to 127. At tea, Hampshire were 140 for 5 and all but home.

Yorkshire 1962. From left to right, back row: E.I. Lester (scorer), P.J. Sharpe, D.E.V. Padgett, M. Ryan, M.J. Cowan, R.K. Platt, D. Wilson, J.B. Bolus, K. Gillhouley, G. Alcock (masseur). Front row: K. Taylor, R. Illingworth, D.B. Close, J.V. Wilson (captain), F.S. Trueman, J.G. Binks, W.B. Stott.

YORKSHIRE v. HAMPSHIRE

Yet there was to be one final twist in this see-saw match. From 156 for 5, the visitor's last five wickets managed only one more run in twenty dramatic minutes against Illingworth's spin and Trueman's pace. Inexplicably, Hampshire had conspired to lose the game by five runs. Illingworth's five wickets had turned the game in dramatic fashion and this narrow and unpredictable win set the tone for the remainder of Yorkshire's season. Despite going unbeaten from 22 June onwards, only a seven-wicket win in their final match against Glamorgan at Harrogate allowed them to reclaim the Championship from Hampshire (who slipped to tenth in the table).

YORKSHIRE v. HAMPSHIRE

Yorkshire won the toss and elected to bat

Umpires: W.E. Phillipson and W.H. Copson

YORKSHIRE

J.B. Bolus	lbw b Heath	31	c Harrison b White	0
K. Taylor	c Gray b Shackleton	1	lbw b Heath	7
P.J. Sharpe	c Horton b White	5	c&b Shackleton	13
D.E.V. Padgett	c Livingstone b Shackleton	10	lbw b Shackleton	5
W.B. Stott	c Harrison b Shackleton	15	b White	21
R. Illingworth	c Sainsbury b Heath	7	c Harrison b White	13
J.V. Wilson*	c Livingstone b Shackleton	51	c Barnard b Shackleton	45
F.S. Trueman	c White b Shackleton	8	c Wassell b Shackleton	41
D. Wilson	c Harrison b Shackleton	19	lbw b Shackleton	4
J.G. Binks+	c Wassell b Shackleton	3	c Wassell b White	12
M.J. Cowan	not out	1	not out	0
Extras		0	(b4 lb9 nb2)	15
TOTAL		151		176

FOW 1st: 7, 18, 41, 49, 63, 75, 85, 130, 148, 151
FOW 2nd: 1, 22, 26, 31, 55, 70, 137, 145, 176, 176

Bowling 1st: Shackleton 31-7-78-7 White 20-4-52-1 Heath 10-3-21-2

Bowling 2nd: Shackleton 34-16-67-5 White 19-5-55-4 Heath 14-3-39-1

HAMPSHIRE

J.R. Gray	b Trueman	9	c Binks b Trueman	78
H. Horton	c Sharpe b Trueman	67	c Binks b Cowan	12
H.M. Barnard	c Sharpe b Trueman	23	b D. Wilson	6
M. Heath	c&b D. Wilson	18	c Trueman b Illingworth	0
D.A. Livingstone	c Sharpe b D. Wilson	12	lbw b Taylor	26
P.J. Sainsbury	c D. Wilson b Taylor	9	lbw b Illingworth	15
A.C.D. Ingleby-Mackenzie*	c Cowan b Taylor	10	c Cowan b Illingworth	8
L. Harrison+	c Binks b Cowan	1	c J.V. Wilson b Illingworth	1
A.R. Wassell	lbw b Trueman	0	not out	0
D. Shackleton	c Sharpe b Trueman	2	b Trueman	0
D.W. White	not out	6	c Trueman b Illingworth	1
Extras	(b4 lb4)	8	(b10)	10
TOTAL		165		157

FOW 1st: 10, 102, 103, 126, 145, 155, 156, 157, 159, 165
FOW 2nd: 28, 41, 97, 127, 135, 156, 156, 156, 157, 157

Bowling 1st: Trueman 23.2-9-34-5 Cowan 24-6-50-1 Taylor 10-5-16-2 Illingworth 6-1-14-0 D. Wilson 8-0-37-2 Bolus 2-1-6-0

Bowling 2nd: Trueman 24-9-49-2 Cowan 17-6-30-1 D. Wilson 13-7-25-1 Illingworth 22-12-33-5 Taylor 5-4-10-1

YORKSHIRE WON BY FIVE RUNS

YORKSHIRE v. WEST INDIANS

Date: 15, 16, 17 May 1963
Location: Middlesbrough

First-class tour match

There were three factors in the 1963 season that contributed to the rejuvenation of Fred Trueman. In the first place, he had cut down his run-up from 17 paces to 12; although this meant that he had lost some speed, he had gained in both control and the ability to make the ball move away late even more effectively. Secondly, Yorkshire had a new captain, in the person of Brian Close, and this move was welcomed by Trueman. During the 1962 season, Vic Wilson, Close's predecessor, had sent Trueman home from Taunton for arriving late and the two never patched up their differences, the fast bowler refusing to contribute to Wilson's leaving present when he retired at the end of that season.

Thirdly, and possibly most importantly, a fine West Indies side had arrived in England. They had taken part in a magnificent Test series in Australia two and a half years previously and had defeated India 5-0 in the following overseas season. They possessed a wonderful array of stroke-players, with, more significantly for Trueman, real rivals in the fast bowling department in the shape of Wes Hall and Charlie Griffith. The former had toured England in 1957 and was now regarded by many (but not by Trueman!) as the world's premier fast bowler. Less was known of Griffith but the threat from him was proven when he fractured the skull of India's captain Nari Contractor when playing for Barbados. The opening batsman never played for his country again.

When the West Indians arrived at Middlesbrough, which was hosting a touring team for the first time, they had won two and drawn two of their first-class matches thus far. Yorkshire had won two (both in the Championship) and drawn three. Trueman had already scored the first century of his career and later, in the match ending on 14 May against Warwickshire at Edgbaston, had match figures of 10 wickets for 36 runs as the home side was bundled out for 35 and 55.

A game against Yorkshire was regarded for decades by various touring teams as a sixth Test match and the visitors' approach was exemplified by the fact that seven of their chosen eleven would play a significant part in the Tests against England. This included captain Frank Worrell, star batsmen Rohan Kanhai and Basil Butcher, the world's best all-rounder in Gary Sobers and Griffith – but not Hall.

Grey skies and cool winds were not to the visitors' liking but they reduced the home side to 95 for 6 in front of a 7,000-strong

West Indies team 1963. From left to right, back row: G. Duckworth (scorer), W.V. Rodriguez, S.M. Nurse, M.C. Carew, C.C. Griffith, L.A. King, E.D.A. St J. McMorris, L.R. Gibbs, B.F. Butcher, D. Pye (masseur). Seated: B. Gaskin (manager), R.B. Kanhai, C.C. Hunte, F.M. Worrell (captain), W.W. Hall, G.S. Sobers, A.L. Valentine, H.L. Burnett (assistant-manager). Front row (on ground): D.L. Murray, J.S. Solomon, D.W. Allan.

crowd. Griffith had also sent John Hampshire back to the pavilion with a very painful knock-out blow on the cheek – an injury that affected him for several years. Bryan Stott and Trueman repaired the situation with an hour-long 78-run stand for the seventh wicket that was duly regarded by Worrell as the game's most telling episode. Stott survived several edged strokes into the slips and Trueman batted with confidence in the knowledge that he would not be subjected to the barrage of bumpers that his higher-order teammates had to contend with. He hit 2 sixes and 6 fours in his 105-minute innings. Stott hit 9 fours in an innings of similar length.

The pitch was proving to be of variable bounce and none of the West Indian batsmen really settled in what were, to them, alien conditions. Although Mel Ryan prised out both openers, it was Trueman and the less-often-used medium pace of Ken Taylor who did most of the damage, exploiting the conditions to full advantage. Opener Worrell top-scored, his stand with 'Joey' Carew for the first wicket of 29 being the highest of the innings, and Yorkshire gained a very significant first-innings lead of 117.

The home side's second innings had reached only three when another batsman had to retire hurt. This time Doug Padgett was hit by Griffith, again on the cheek, and took no further part in the match. Both Padgett and Hampshire later stated that Griffith was the fastest bowler that either of them had ever faced. He aroused much controversy over the course of the season and for decades afterwards as several batsmen accused Griffith of throwing his bouncer and yorker. Although he later led his side's Test series bowling averages and was the West Indians' leading wicket-taker in both the Tests and all matches, there has always remained doubt as to the fairness in his delivery. Trueman himself reasoned that such a change in pace could not be otherwise gained from what was an ambling approach to the wicket by such a burly man.

John Hampshire – knocked out by a ball from Griffith, he later returned to the crease to complete his innings.

Worrell eschewed the use of his spinners and took four wickets himself with his own brand of cutters delivered at a similar speed to that of Taylor. Nevertheless, Close was able to declare Yorkshire's second innings with only six wickets down and set the visitors 263 to win. Trueman was left 20 not out and his total of 75 runs was the most by any batsman in the match. Worrell sent in David Allan and then Griffith, as nightwatchmen, to partner Carew, but the ploy, as well as an appeal against the light, failed.

The final morning dawned just as gloomy as it had on the first two days. Trueman again took the wicket of Kanhai with a perfect out-swinger – pitching on middle and taking the off bail. Seymour Nurse and Sobers took up the challenge and added 46 in fifty minutes; Butcher also batted in the only way he knew and hit 30 of his 46 runs in boundaries. However, the cloudy conditions and the soft pitch were once again exploited to the full by Trueman. His occasional use of the bouncer – as a surprise weapon – was in direct contrast to that of Griffith and he bowled with skill and intelligence. With the ball swinging prodigiously, he took five wickets for the second time, finishing with match figures of 10 for 81. It was his greatest all-round

YORKSHIRE v. WEST INDIANS

match – the only time in his career that he scored a half-century and took ten wickets in the same game. The contest ended twelve minutes before lunch. In a most embarrassing defeat the West Indians had lost 19 wickets for a total of 260 runs and only one batsman had passed 30 in either innings.

Yorkshire remained the only county to defeat the 1963 West Indies side in a first-class match. They lost one of the Test matches and a one-day game against Sussex, the Gillette Cup winners, at the end of the tour. They were one of the most popular and successful squads to visit the British Isles but Middlesbrough in May and a fired-up Trueman were too much for their stars.

Meanwhile, Trueman's season just got better and better. He later scored another century and took ten wickets in a match five times – three of these being against the West Indians. He led the first-class averages at the end of the season as well as England's Test averages in taking 34 wickets – more than twice as many as that of his nearest rival. This tally remains the record for a series in England against the West Indies. At the age of thirty-two he was in his pomp.

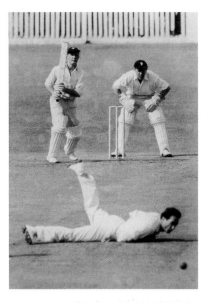

Bryan Stott (batting here against Kent at Gravesend in 1960) added 78 in an hour with Trueman for Yorkshire's seventh wicket.

Fred Trueman hits out for the Players v. Gentlemen at Lord's in 1962. At Middlesbrough in 1963 he had a fine all-round match against the tourists with ten wickets, two catches and a half century in Yorkshire's first innings.

YORKSHIRE v. WEST INDIANS

Yorkshire won the toss and elected to bat

Umpires: N. Oldfield and H. Yarnold

YORKSHIRE

D.E.V. Padgett	c Allan b King	5	retired hurt		2
J.H. Hampshire	b King	19	c Solomon b Worrell		25
P.J. Sharpe	lbw b Griffith	20	lbw b King		10
D.B. Close*	b Griffith	23	lbw b Worrell		23
K. Taylor	lbw b Griffith	10	c Allan b Worrell		13
W.B. Stott	c Kanhai b Valentine	65	b Griffith		8
R. Illingworth	c Allan b King	1	c King b Worrell		28
F.S. Trueman	c Allan b Griffith	55	not out		20
D. Wilson	b Sobers	4			
J.G. Binks+	b Griffith	14	(9) not out		13
M. Ryan	not out	5			
Extras	(lb5)	5	(lb2 w1)		3
TOTAL		226	(6 wkts dec)		145

FOW 1st: 13, 50, 61, 66, 85, 95, 173, 187, 219, 226
FOW 2nd: 32, 50, 72, 77, 105, 119

Bowling 1st: Griffith 22.2-7-37-5 King 22-4-67-3 Worrell 9-1-19-0 Valentine 17-3-48-1 Sobers 8-1-50-1

Bowling 2nd: Griffith 19-9-33-1 King 20-3-47-1 Worrell 20-3-62-4

WEST INDIANS

F.M.M. Worrell*	c Close b Ryan	22	(9) b Trueman	18
M.C. Carew	c Taylor b Ryan	8	c Illingworth b Ryan	3
R.B. Kanhai	b Trueman	19	(4) b Trueman	9
S.M. Nurse	c Binks b Trueman	7	(5) b Illingworth	26
G. St. A. Sobers	c Trueman b Taylor	17	(6) b Taylor	29
B.F. Butcher	c Binks b Taylor	13	(7) not out	46
J.S. Solomon	c Sharpe b Taylor	4	(8) c Hampshire b Trueman	12
D.W. Allan+	not out	16	(1) c Trueman b Ryan	0
C.C. Griffith	hit wkt b Trueman	2	(3) c Binks b Trueman	4
L.A. King	c Taylor b Trueman	0	b Trueman	4
A.L. Valentine	c Close b Trueman	0	absent hurt	
Extras	(lb1)	1		0
TOTAL		109		151

FOW 1st: 20, 37, 56, 57, 75, 79, 100, 103, 103, 109
FOW 2nd: 1, 6, 8, 26, 71, 71, 110, 147, 151

Bowling 1st: Trueman 20-5-38-5 Ryan 25-11-32-2 Taylor 26-12-33-3 Illingworth 2-1-4-0 Close 1-0-1-0

Bowling 2nd: Trueman 13.3-5-43-5 Ryan 14-3-52-2 Illingworth 12-4-42-1 Taylor 11-5-14-1

YORKSHIRE WON BY 111 RUNS

YORKSHIRE v. SURREY

Date: 4 September 1965   Gillette Cup final
Location: Lord's

In a damp season that saw Worcestershire crowned County Champions for a second consecutive season, Yorkshire salvaged some pride – having finished fourth in the Championship and having suffered the indignity of being dismissed for their lowest ever first-class total (23) against Hampshire at Middlesbrough – by winning the recently introduced (1963) 60-over one-day Gillette Cup competition.

Yorkshire's path to Lord's came via comfortable wins over Leicestershire and Somerset and a close-fought 20-run triumph over Warwickshire. Surrey, led by Micky Stewart, were Yorkshire's final opponents in this new format of the game on a warm early September day in front of a 25,000 strong crowd. Persistent rain had preceded the final. The Lord's groundsman Ted Swannell and his staff worked wonders to get the arena dry and ready for play at 12.15p.m. Stewart won the toss and, somewhat surprisingly in view of the wet conditions, put Yorkshire into bat. At first, though, the decision seemed justified. After the first 10 overs, Geoff Arnold and David Sydenham had restricted Yorkshire to 20 without loss. Stewart reasoned that the batting side would struggle on the wet surface and runs would be hard to come by on the slow outfield.

Ken Taylor was the first wicket to fall, caught by Ken Barrington for nine, and the captain Brian Close took it upon himself to come in at no.3. Close's promotion to no.3 was to combat Surrey's left-arm bowler Sydenham who had bowled well against the right-handed batsmen of Yorkshire in the Championship fixture at Bradford earlier that season. Together the left-handed Close and Geoff Boycott added 192 for the second wicket at a furious rate. Boycott's early defensive approach was cast aside as he 'played forcing shots all round the wicket', commented *Wisden*. When Close departed for 79, Fred Trueman and John Hampshire continued the aggressive approach. Boycott's normally thoughtful, technically correct defensive style was replaced by an offensive and belligerent method. His first century of the season (also the first in the Gillette Cup that year) reached 146 before the end came in the fifty-fifth over. In all his innings lasted just under three and a half hours and contained 3 sixes and 15 fours. Yorkshire's total of 317 for 4 remained the highest in the competition final until 1993 when both Sussex and Warwickshire exceeded it in the same match! Lacking a spinner (Pat Pocock probably), Ron Tindall and Barrington made up eight overs at a cost of 90 runs.

Gordon Ross wrote in *Playfair Cricket Monthly*: 'Surrey were obviously affected psychologically by the magnitude of their task which was never "on" from the word go.' So it proved,

Boycott hitting out during his innings of 146 watched on by wicketkeeper Arnold Long and Ken Barrington at slip.

for although Stewart (33) and Tindall (57) batted with spirit, the loss of three wickets in the ninth over to Fred Trueman (three wickets with four balls) signalled no way back for the beaten southern county. Illingworth's five wickets included three wickets in four balls as five of the Surrey batsmen managed just one run between them. They lost three wickets on 27 and another hat-trick of batsmen at 76. There was no way back: all out for 142, Surrey were beaten by the comprehensive margin of 175 runs in a mostly one-sided final. Brian Close received the trophy from 'Gubby' Allen and the chairman of the England selectors, Doug Insole, had an easy task in presenting the bespectacled Boycott (who had been dropped from the Test side by Insole) with the Man of the Match award. John Arlott was heard to say on his radio commentary that day: 'Boycott has enjoyed himself, surprised himself, and at times, nearly rocked himself off his feet with the power of his shots. And this from a man who has already become a legendary stonewaller.'

YORKSHIRE v. SURREY

Surrey won the toss and elected to field

Umpires: J.S. Buller and C.S. Elliott

YORKSHIRE

G. Boycott	c Storey b Barrington	146
K. Taylor	c Barrington b Sydenham	9
D.B. Close*	c Edrich b Gibson	79
F.S. Trueman	b Arnold	24
J.H. Hampshire	not out	38
D. Wilson	not out	11
D.E.V. Padgett		
P.J. Sharpe		
R. Illingworth		
R.A. Hutton		
J.G. Binks+		
Extras	(b3 lb4 nb3)	10
TOTAL	(4 wkts, 60 overs)	317

FOW: 22, 214, 248, 292

Bowling: Arnold 13-3-51-1 Sydenham 13-1-67-1 Gibson 13-1-66-1 Storey 13-2-33-0 Tindall 3-0-36-0 Barrington 5-0-54-1

SURREY

M.J. Stewart*	st Binks b Wilson	33
J.H. Edrich	c Illingworth b Trueman	15
W.A. Smith	lbw b Trueman	0
K.F. Barrington	c Binks b Trueman	0
R.A.E. Tindall	c Wilson b Close	57
S.J. Storey	lbw b Illingworth	1
M.J. Edwards	b Illingworth	0
D. Gibson	lbw b Illingworth	0
A. Long+	b Illingworth	17
G.G. Arnold	not out	3
D.A.D. Sydenham	b Illingworth	8
Extras	(b4 lb4)	8
TOTAL	(40.4 overs)	142

FOW: 27, 27, 27, 75, 76, 76, 76, 130, 132, 142

Bowling: Trueman 9-0-31-3 Hutton 8-3-17-0 Wilson 9-0-45-1 Illingworth 11.4-1-29-5 Close 3-0-12-1

YORKSHIRE WON BY 175 RUNS

YORKSHIRE v. GLOUCESTERSHIRE

Date: 6, 7 September 1967

County Championship

Location: Harrogate

Yorkshire went into their final Championship game of the season in third position but only two points behind Kent and Leicestershire, both of whom had completed their programmes. With four points available for first-innings lead, that was all that would be needed for the home side to clinch its twenty-eighth outright title.

Yorkshire had won only three of their previous thirteen matches but, more significantly, their captain Brian Close had been 'severely censured' by the MCC and stripped of the England captaincy. This was the result of time-wasting tactics against Warwickshire just eighteen days previously. Feelings of resentment against the game's establishment were reflected when Peter West of *The Times* was subjected to chants and ironic applause from spectators in the main stand. He had taken part in a television debate opposite Michael Parkinson on the subject of 'The Close Affair'.

Meanwhile, the home side had been asked to bat on a soft pitch that should have proved difficult for batting. However, the drying process was delayed by showers and Geoff Boycott and Phil Sharpe batted well enough to post a century opening stand. In due course, the spinners came on and wickets began to fall so much so that the next four batsmen could manage only 15 runs between them. Ray Illingworth supported the tail and the day ended with Yorkshire on 245 for 9.

The large second-day crowd that had gathered was immediately entertained by a last-wicket stand between Fred Trueman and Don Wilson. The pair scored 64 runs in only thirty-five minutes, both players indulging themselves in some powerful hitting. Gloucestershire began their reply well and at the lunch interval had progressed promisingly to 66 for 0. This meant that 130 runs had come in the morning session for the loss of only one wicket.

The rest of the day was in complete contrast as 20 wickets fell for just 167 runs. The combination of Illingworth and Wilson together with a drying pitch proved far too much for the West Country team. Once Arthur Milton had departed, the remainder of the day became a procession. Although Ron Nicholls compiled an assured half-century, five first-innings 'ducks' told their own story and he was run out attempting to retain the strike. Yorkshire had a first-innings lead of 175 and the celebrations could begin.

By now the crowd had grown even larger in the hope of witnessing a conclusive victory inside two days. Play was delayed for a while after the tea interval as several spectators had spilled over onto the grass beyond the boundary and in the absence of stewards it was the players who had to do the necessary cajoling in order that play could resume.

The visitors' second innings was even more pitiful than their first effort had been and Illingworth's bowling, supported by some

Brian Close leads off his victorious side after their Championship-securing win over Gloucestershire to the acclaim of the Harrogate crowd.

YORKSHIRE v. GLOUCESTERSHIRE

brilliant catching, had become virtually unplayable. Not only did he again take seven wickets but conceded only six runs in doing so as Close took the option of the extra half-hour and the match concluded at 6.45p.m. Celebratory photographs duly showed a battle scar as Close, who had been struck on the head earlier in the day when fielding in his usual suicidal short-leg position, was sporting a huge plaster.

This triumph meant that Yorkshire had now won six titles in nine seasons and the current squad could bear comparison with those illustrious teams of earlier decades. Writing afterwards, Close stated that he had felt that, following the controversy, the whole team had been keyed up to support him with a really great effort to end the season on a high.

YORKSHIRE v. GLOUCESTERSHIRE

Gloucestershire won the toss and elected to field

Umpires: A. Gaskell and R.S. Lay

YORKSHIRE

G. Boycott	b Bissex	74
P.J. Sharpe	c Russell b Bissex	75
D.E.V. Padgett	c Mortimore b Allen	6
J.H. Hampshire	c&b Allen	0
K. Taylor	c Shepherd b Bissex	9
D.B. Close*	b Bissex	0
R. Illingworth	b A.S. Brown	46
R.A. Hutton	c Milton b Mortimore	7
J.G. Binks+	lbw b Mortimore	8
D. Wilson	not out	39
F.S. Trueman	c D. Brown b Mortimore	34
Extras	(lb9 w1 nb1)	11
TOTAL		309

FOW 1st: 127, 151, 157, 159, 159, 179, 211, 229, 245, 309

Bowling 1st: A.S. Brown 28-5-78-1 Windows 10-0-47-0 Mortimore 25.1-6-45-3 Allen 24-6-62-2 Bissex 28-9-66-4

GLOUCESTERSHIRE

R.B. Nicholls	run out	52	c Padgett b Illingworth		16
C.A. Milton	c Sharpe b Wilson	22	b Hutton		16
S.E. Russell	lbw b Illingworth	0	st Binks b Illingworth		16
D. Brown	lbw b Illingworth	0	c Wilson b Illingworth		1
A.S. Brown	c Binks b Illingworth	0	lbw b Close		15
D. Shepherd	c Trueman b Illingworth	12	c Trueman b Illingworth		0
M. Bissex	lbw b Wilson	29	c Trueman b Illingworth		1
J.B. Mortimore*	b Illingworth	0	c Trueman b Illingworth		0
D.A. Allen	lbw b Illingworth	12	not out		5
A.R. Windows	lbw b Illingworth	0	c Hampshire b Illingworth		13
B.J. Meyer+	not out	4	b Close		8
Extras	(lb2 nb1)	3	(lb8)		8
TOTAL		134			99

FOW 1st: 66, 67, 67, 71, 81, 96, 96, 118, 118, 134
FOW 2nd: 24, 38, 41, 52, 52, 64, 66, 72, 89, 99

Bowling 1st: Trueman 4-0-17-0 Hutton 3-0-8-0 Wilson 20.4-6-41-2 Illingworth 23-8-58-7 Close 4-1-7-0

Bowling 2nd: Trueman 7-1-25-0 Hutton 5-2-10-1 Wilson 7-3-12-0 Illingworth 13-9-6-7 Close 7.5-2-38-2

YORKSHIRE WON BY AN INNINGS AND 76 RUNS

YORKSHIRE v. AUSTRALIANS

Date: 29 June, 1, 2 July 1968   First-class tour match

Location: Bramall Lane, Sheffield

The twenty-fifth Australian party to tour the United Kingdom – under the captaincy of Bill Lawry – were plagued by poor weather throughout the rain-ruined summer of 1968. They were the youngest squad Australia had sent to England; eight of the tourists were twenty-five or under when the trip got underway. Yet, despite a modest final tour record of ten wins in twenty-nine matches played (16 draws and one abandoned fixture being reflective of the bad weather), they suffered only three defeats and shared the Test rubber (1-1) with England to retain the Ashes. The Australians excelled in the field with Paul Sheahan, Ian Redpath and Doug Walters outstanding. Johnny Gleeson, with his leg-breaks, took most wickets during the tour, although tall off-spinner Ashley Mallett looked a good prospect. Amongst the batsmen, only Redpath and South Australian newcomer Ian Chappell passed 1,000 tour runs.

One-nil up in the Test series and unbeaten to that point on the trip, Australia announced eight of the side that had played in the drawn Second Test against England at Lord's for their fixture with the reigning County Champions at Bramall Lane. Right-arm fast bowler David Renneberg, reserve wicketkeeper Brian Taber and batsman John Inverarity made up the Australian XI. Yorkshire were led by their veteran (thirty-seven) fast bowler Fred Trueman in the absence of the injured Brian Close. Geoff Boycott returned from Test duty and, other than the inexperienced bowler Peter Stringer, Yorkshire fielded a full-strength side.

Acting-captain Trueman won the toss and decided to give his batsmen first use of a 'slow Bramall Lane wicket' against the Aussie Test quick bowlers Graham McKenzie and Alan Connolly. A Saturday crowd at the Lane of 9,500 saw Boycott and Phil Sharpe, on a pitch, according to *Wisden*, 'that gave some, but certainly not excessive help to both fast bowling and slow', compile a 105-run opening partnership in 165 minutes before Sharpe was removed by Gleeson for 47. Yorkshire's middle-order of Doug Padgett, John Hampshire and Ken Taylor all made solid contributions without going onto a big score, whilst Boycott, familiar with the opposition bowling, anchored the innings with 86 (1 six, 10 fours) in 230 minutes. Trueman,

bent on beating the tourists, chose to continue batting on the second morning from an overnight score of 271 for 4. Eighty-four further runs were added in eighty-five minutes. Ray Illingworth's 69 not out (1 six and 7 fours) helped Yorkshire to 355 before the declaration came forty minutes before lunch. McKenzie and Gleeson, with four wickets each, were the most successful of the Australian bowlers.

Turning back the years, Trueman opened the bowling

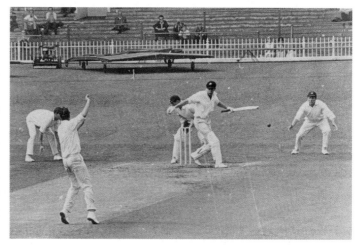

Australian captain Bill Lawry pads away a delivery from Yorkshire's Don Wilson. Jimmy Binks is behind the wicket, Phil Sharpe at slip and John Hampshire close in on the left of the picture.

off his youthful long run and he and Richard Hutton quickly reduced Australia to 50 for 3. 'Captain Trueman' played his full part in the Australians' first-innings decline. Redpath was caught behind by Jimmy Binks off his bowling, with the score on 26, and he caught both Walters and Sheahan off Hutton and Lawry (the only player to pass 50) off Illingworth's off-spin; he ran out Chappell with a throw from cover and came back at the end of the innings to pick up the last two wickets (Gleeson and Connolly), both bowled. Trueman ended with figures of 3 for 32 from 10.2 overs of his one-time best. Illingworth spun out the lower middle-order and Australia found themselves batting again twenty minutes before the close with a first-innings deficit of 207. The final wound in a thoroughly painful day for the tourists was applied by Hutton who bowled Lawry for a duck. Australia were 15 for 1 going into the final day with the one batsman perhaps capable of batting out time for a draw already back in the pavilion.

At first it seemed that the weather might save the Australians' unbeaten record when a thunderstorm, characteristic of the humid weather that week, delayed the start of play for twenty minutes. In other parts of the county the storms were the worst recorded in many a year but Yorkshire's fortunes were such that no other rain delays were suffered on that historic Tuesday, 2 July. With the storm passed and the surface dried it was Hutton again who made the early breakthrough, having Redpath, playing no shot, lbw for 12. Walters and Sheahan put on an 'uneasy' 40 before Trueman returned for a second spell and 'produced a devastating thunderbolt' to knock over Sheahan's middle stump. Chappell, though, kept good company

McKenzie is caught behind by Binks off Trueman for nought in the Australians' second innings.

YORKSHIRE v. AUSTRALIANS

with Walters ('looking immovable') and they added a further 50 for the fourth wicket before Illingworth held a catch at gully, again off Trueman, to end Walters' battling innings of 62 soon after lunch. The next three wickets fell for only two runs as Illingworth's spin again 'caused batting misgivings' in the Australian ranks – 113 for 7. Illingworth's fourth victim was Gleeson, bowled for 12; McKenzie was caught behind off the tireless Trueman without scoring. When Connolly, sweeping at Don Wilson, was run out by Hampshire's quick return from short leg, Yorkshire had obtained their first victory against an Australian side since 1902 by an innings and 69 runs. The match ended, as Trueman had casually and uncannily forecast at a press conference that morning, at 3.30p.m. on the final afternoon.

Afterwards, the Australian manager Bob Parrish was generous in defeat: 'Yorkshire outplayed us all the way. They played better cricket than we did and thoroughly deserved to win...' J.M. Kilburn wrote of the notable victory: '...the Australians were neither a ready sacrifice nor an innocent victim. Yorkshire had to undertake the hardest of work to win with apparent ease.' *Wisden* praised the style of the county's play: 'Yorkshire gave an impressive display of purposeful cricket.' For Trueman, in what transpired to be his final season as a Yorkshire player, victory over Australia was the crowning glory in a considerable playing career. Indeed, writing much later he described it as 'the best moment in my cricketing life'. He rightly won lasting praise for the way he led the side to victory at Bramall Lane and sadly it would be the last such epic encounter against the Australians at the Sheffield venue. The 1968 Australians' only other defeats came against Glamorgan in early August (by 79 runs), and in the fifth Test at The Oval when Derek Underwood spun England to victory by 226 runs with only minutes to spare. Yorkshire finished the summer as County Champions, a feat also achieved by their Second XI team. The Australian triumph at Sheffield by Trueman and his men crowned one of the truly great seasons in the club's history.

Tourists were outplayed all round

Above: The newspaper headlines celebrate Yorkshire's historic innings win against Australia, 2 July 1968 – the county's first triumph over the Aussies for sixty-six years.

Left: The architect of the Australians' demise at Sheffield – Yorkshire captain Fred Trueman.

YORKSHIRE v. AUSTRALIANS

YORKSHIRE v. AUSTRALIANS

Yorkshire won the toss and elected to bat

Umpires: R. Aspinall and T.W. Spencer

YORKSHIRE

G. Boycott	c Taber b Chappell	86
P.J. Sharpe	c Lawry b Gleeson	47
D.E.V. Padgett	st Taber b Gleeson	56
J.H. Hampshire	c Lawry b Gleeson	33
K. Taylor	c Taber b McKenzie	24
R. Illingworth	not out	69
J.G. Binks+	c Taber b McKenzie	0
R.A. Hutton	c Walters b McKenzie	2
F.S. Trueman*	c Sheahan b Gleeson	13
D. Wilson	c Redpath b McKenzie	0
P. Stringer	not out	12
Extras	(lb6 w1 nb6)	13
TOTAL	(9 wkts dec)	355

FOW: 105, 162, 219, 230, 287, 287, 297, 330, 330

Bowling: McKenzie 27-7-73-4 Renneburg 19-2-58-0 Connolly 32-16-49-0 Gleeson 47-12-123-4 Chappell 6-0-33-1 Walters 7-5-6-0

AUSTRALIANS

W.M. Lawry*	c Trueman b Illingworth	58	b Hutton	0
I.R. Redpath	c Binks b Trueman	12	lbw b Hutton	12
K.D. Walters	c Trueman b Hutton	4	c Illingworth b Trueman	62
A.P. Sheahan	c Trueman b Hutton	10	b Trueman	17
I.M. Chappell	run out	18	c Hutton b Illingworth	26
R.J. Inverarity	c Stringer b Illingworth	2	lbw b Illingworth	1
H.B. Taber+	b Illingworth	9	st Binks b Illingworth	0
G.D. McKenzie	c Hutton b Illingworth	6	c Binks b Trueman	0
J.W. Gleeson	b Trueman	4	b Illingworth	12
A.N. Connolly	b Trueman	20	run out	0
D.E. Renneberg	not out	0	not out	4
Extras	(lb2 w1 nb2)	5	(lb2 w1 nb1)	4
TOTAL		148		138

FOW 1st: 26, 36, 50, 97, 99, 113, 119, 123, 147, 148
FOW 2nd: 8, 21, 61, 111, 112, 112, 113, 130, 134, 138

Bowling 1st: Trueman 10.2-2-32-3 Hutton 12-3-37-2 Stringer 4-2-6-0 Illingworth 17-3-44-4 Wilson 9-1-20-0 Taylor 1-0-4-0

Bowling 2nd: Trueman 19-4-51-3 Hutton 12-5-35-2 Illingworth 22-12-23-4 Wilson 13.1-7-25-0 Boycott 1-1-0-0

YORKSHIRE WON BY AN INNINGS AND 69 RUNS

DERBYSHIRE v. YORKSHIRE

Date: 6 September 1969   Gillette Cup final
Location: Lord's

In some ways this was a repeat of Yorkshire's only previous Gillette Cup final appearance. Their opponents won the toss and asked Yorkshire to bat; skipper Brian Close took part in the highest partnership of the game; Yorkshire won the match with spin taking most of the wickets. There the similarities ended.

Derbyshire had reached their first final on the backs of their bowlers and Derek Morgan's decision to field first was taken in the knowledge that they were more likely to be at their most effective in the morning session. It was not to be so. The day was warm and sunny and the young Yorkshire openers, both of whom were uncapped, batted with comfort from the outset.

Geoff Boycott had suffered a broken hand in the previous Championship game and had been ruled out of the match. Barrie Leadbeater was also injured in the same game but his broken finger was strapped up and he was to play the most famous innings of his largely unfulfilled career. He lost his partner John Woodford to a catch at the wicket after a 39-run stand and was then joined by Close. Together the pair took Yorkshire past the 100 mark – achieved after 30 overs – with a mixture of care (Leadbeater) and aggression (Close). The latter played some powerful attacking strokes including a massive six off Morgan but perished in advancing down the wicket to Alan Ward – the fastest bowler in the country.

Thereafter, the match was something of an anti-climax. Leadbeater went on to make the highest score of the game, scoring more than twice as many runs as his nearest rival but only Doug Padgett and Richard Hutton made much of an impression in the remainder of Yorkshire's innings. After being 103 for 1, a closing score of 219 for 8 had to be seen as something of a disappointment, although it was widely assumed that it would be enough. The Derbyshire bowlers had stuck well to the task, Ian Buxton being the most economical, Ward the most penetrative.

Derbyshire's innings began with a good opening stand but the runs were scored too slowly against a well-set field. Time and time again the batsmen made an attacking stroke only for the ball to go straight to a fielder. Close was at his most inspiring. He had batted by example and now he did the same in bowling, taking over from Old for the thirteenth over of the innings, and fielding as well as captaining with vigour and enthusiasm. Just before the tea interval, Peter Gibbs, in desperation, swung at Tony Nicholson – who was to bowl his 12 overs straight through for only 14 runs – and was clean bowled.

The first wicket stand of 37 was to be Derbyshire's best

Brian Close and his Yorkshire teammates celebrate their Gillette Cup final victory at Lord's. From left to right: A.G. Nicholson, R.A. Hutton, D.B. Close, J.G. Binks, P.J. Sharpe, D. Wilson, J.H. Hampshire.

effort as wickets fell regularly throughout the remainder of the innings. The game progressed with an air of inevitability partly because Mick Page, the best stroke player, had to bat lower in the order after suffering a side-strain when fielding. Buxton held things up for a while, top-scoring with 34, but no one could stay with him for long and the innings concluded with more than five overs remaining. Close had taken three wickets, two catches and played throughout with a determination that would ensure that the trophy would return to his county.

It was Leadbeater, however, who won the Man of the Match award. In fourteen seasons with Yorkshire he made only one first-class century but later became a well-respected umpire on the county circuit as well as standing in five one-day internationals. But a cup final at Lord's in 1969 was his finest hour.

DERBYSHIRE v. YORKSHIRE

Derbyshire won the toss and elected to field

Umpires: T.W. Spencer and H. Yarnold

YORKSHIRE

B. Leadbeater	c Taylor b Ward	76
J.D. Woodford	c Taylor b Eyre	15
D.B. Close*	c Page b Ward	37
P.J. Sharpe	b Ward	3
D.E.V. Padgett	c Buxton b Rumsey	30
J.H. Hampshire	c Morgan b Rhodes	2
R.A. Hutton	not out	29
J.G. Binks+	b Rhodes	4
D. Wilson	c Ward b Rumsey	2
C.M. Old	not out	3
A.G. Nicholson		
Extras	(b3 lb13 nb2)	18
TOTAL	(8 wkts, 60 overs)	219

FOW: 39, 103, 107, 154, 157, 177, 192, 195

Bowling: Ward 12-1-31-3 Rhodes 12-2-47-2 Buxton 12-6-24-0 Eyre 12-0-53-1 Rumsey 11-0-33-2 Morgan 1-0-13-0

DERBYSHIRE

P.J.K. Gibbs	b Nicholson	19
D.H.K. Smith	b Close	26
D.C. Morgan*	run out	5
A. Ward	c Close b Hutton	17
I.R. Buxton	c Close b Wilson	34
J.F. Harvey	b Wilson	3
M.H. Page	c Wilson b Close	16
R.W. Taylor+	c Leadbeater b Close	2
T.J.P. Eyre	not out	14
F.E. Rumsey	b Wilson	1
H.J. Rhodes	c Hampshire b Old	6
Extras	(b1 lb4 w2)	7
TOTAL	(54.4 overs)	150

FOW: 37, 49, 54, 77, 83, 112, 128, 129, 136, 150

Bowling: Old 9.4-1-25-1 Nicholson 12-5-14-1 Close 11-2-36-3 Wilson 12-0-38-3 Hutton 10-1-30-1

YORKSHIRE WON BY 69 RUNS

YORKSHIRE v. MIDDLESEX

Date: 8, 10, 11 September 1973   County Championship
Location: Bradford

The year of 1973 witnessed an all-time low for Yorkshire cricket in many respects. In mid-summer the mighty Wilfred Rhodes passed away. A few months earlier another of the inter-war greats, wicketkeeper Arthur Wood, had died and by the close of the year the club had also lost its president, Sir William Worsley. Sheffield's Bramall Lane staged its final county fixture and on the field Yorkshire suffered an embarrassing exit from the Gillette Cup at the hands of Minor County Durham. The County Championship campaign brought little solace for Geoff Boycott's men and they dropped to their lowest-ever position (fourteenth) in the table following their final match against Middlesex (who finished just one place higher) at Bradford.

Whilst this end-of-season fixture between two modest sides had little to recommend it in advance, it did produce only the second tied match in Yorkshire's history. The home side gave a debut to seventeen-year-old Graham Stevenson and the young right-arm medium-fast bowler exploited the helpful conditions on the opening day picking up the wickets of the Middlesex captain Mike Brearley and Clive Radley. Stalwart seam bowler Tony Nicholson was at his best with the ball, picking up 5 for 23 as the visitors managed just 102 all out. Yorkshire were quickly in equal strife. At the close of the first day, 19 wickets had fallen and Yorkshire ('shambling and unsteady' according to the *Yorkshire Post*) had a slim four-run advantage.

Over the weekend, a mystery flu-type virus descended amongst the White Rose bowling contingent. Yorkshire had little option but to declare. Both seamers, Howard Cooper (unable to make it to the ground) and Arthur Robinson (sent home fifteen minutes before the start of play), were unable to bowl in Middlesex's second innings and the debutant Stevenson was forced to retire after bowling only ten overs. Yorkshire had as many as four substitutes on the field at certain stages of the day. Meanwhile, Nicholson and slow left-armer Don Wilson carried the depleted Yorkshire attack. Between them they somehow managed to limit the victory target to 208, with only Brearley (83) truly able to shake off the demons in the Bradford pitch. With no Boycott to master the difficult surface, Yorkshire were relying on stand-in captain Phil Sharpe, Richard Lumb and John Hampshire to provide a solid platform to their second-innings run chase. They made just 16 between them; and so Yorkshire were 54 for 3. Colin Johnson and wicketkeeper/batsman David Bairstow (playing with three stitches in a cut lip) began the fight back and, by the close of the second day's play, the pair had guided Yorkshire to the calmer waters of 121 for 3.

All eleven Yorkshire players were at the ground on the final morning with Cooper and Robinson summoned from their sickbeds, hoping that they wouldn't

Tony Nicholson – 5 for 23 in Middlesex's first innings and 8 for 61 in the match.

YORKSHIRE v. MIDDLESEX

be required. The Johnson/Bairstow fourth-wicket stand, however, ended on 80 and when Mike Selvey removed Stevenson for one to claim his fifth wicket, Yorkshire still needed 62 for victory with only four wickets in hand. Fred Titmus now stepped up to remove Don Wilson, Nicholson and Mike Bore. When the two flu victims Cooper and Robinson came together with nine wickets down, a further 16 were needed for a now unlikely Yorkshire win. Somehow the pair gathered all but one of the necessary runs before chief destroyer Selvey returned to the Middlesex attack and with the fifth ball of his twenty-sixth over uprooted Robinson's middle stump to end what had started as a relatively meaningless final Championship fixture in a thrilling tie.

YORKSHIRE v. MIDDLESEX

Yorkshire won the toss and elected to field

Umpires: H. Horton and G.H. Pope

MIDDLESEX

M.J. Smith	c Bairstow b Nicholson	10	c Wilson b Nicholson		23
N.G. Featherstone	c Hampshire b Nicholson	7	c Lumb b Stevenson		18
J.M. Brearley*	c Bairstow b Stevenson	2	c Sharpe b Wilson		83
C.T. Radley	c Lumb b Stevenson	19	lbw b Bore		18
L.A. Gomes	lbw b Nicholson	12	lbw b Nicholson		0
J.T. Murray+	c Stevenson b Nicholson	21	c&b Wilson		20
P.H. Edmonds	lbw b Cooper	2	c sub b Wilson		9
F.J. Titmus	b Cooper	0	run out		17
K.V. Jones	c Johnson b Cooper	4	c Sharpe b Nicholson		8
C.J.R. Black	lbw b Nicholson	10	c sub b Wilson		4
M.W.W. Selvey	not out	0	not out		0
Extras	(b10 lb2 w1 nb2)	15	(b3 lb2 w4 nb2)		11
TOTAL		102			211

FOW 1st: 14, 19, 41, 44, 77, 82, 82, 92, 92, 102
FOW 2nd: 33, 51, 116, 117, 155, 171, 185, 190, 211, 211

Bowling 1st: Nicholson 15.5-8-23-5 Cooper 17-9-20-3 Stevenson 9-3-23-2 Robinson 7-1-21-0

Bowling 2nd: Nicholson 17.5-3-38-3 Stevenson 10-2-27-1 Wilson 19-5-67-4 Bore 25-9-51-1 Johnson 9-4-17-0

YORKSHIRE

P.J. Sharpe*	c Edmonds b Black	19	c Featherstone b Selvey		4
R.G. Lumb	c Murray b Jones	0	c Jones b Selvey		0
C. Johnson	lbw b Gomes	33	c Radley b Selvey		78
J.H. Hampshire	b Gomes	21	b Titmus		12
D.L. Bairstow+	c Selvey b Titmus	6	b Selvey		56
G.B. Stevenson	c Black b Titmus	7	b Selvey		1
D. Wilson	c Radley b Gomes	0	c Edmonds b Titmus		15
H.P. Cooper	not out	5	not out		10
A.G. Nicholson	lbw b Gomes	0	st Murray b Titmus		2
M.K. Bore	run out	5	b Titmus		9
A.L. Robinson	not out	0	b Selvey		6
Extras	(b4 lb2 nb4)	10	(b4 lb5 w1 nb4)		14
TOTAL	(9 wkts dec)	106			207

FOW 1st: 0, 32, 75, 88, 88, 95, 95, 95, 106
FOW 2nd: 4, 18, 54, 134, 146, 170, 178, 186, 192, 207

Bowling 1st: Selvey 13-6-16-0 Jones 12-4-26-1 Black 5-1-12-1 Edmonds 1-0-6-0 Gomes 18-9-22-4 Titmus 15-8-14-2

Bowling 2nd: Selvey 25.5-5-74-6 Jones 7-3-19-0 Titmus 15-1-41-4 Gomes 15-4-39-0 Edmonds 8-4-20-0

MATCH TIED

YORKSHIRE v. MIDDLESEX

Date: 10, 12, 13 July 1976   County Championship

Location: Bradford

The circumstances surrounding this game were such that no one could have predicted its outcome, let alone the way in which the eventual result was achieved. In the Championship race that constituted the 1976 campaign, Middlesex had thus far gained six victories to Yorkshire's one. Moreover, five of those wins had come in the visitors' last six matches.

To aggravate the situation, Yorkshire were without two injured Test players in Geoff Boycott and Chris Old, as well as Barrie Leadbeater, who had been injured in a car accident. The consequence was that this was one of the most inexperienced teams ever to have represented Yorkshire in the entire history of the County Championship. The side contained only four capped players and only three of the remainder would eventually be deemed good enough to gain caps during their playing careers.

In due course, this match, unbelievably so given the background, was a most closely-fought contest and eventually produced the narrowest win in the history of Yorkshire's first-class cricket. The most dramatic circumstances in which it was achieved also defy logical analysis. It was a pulsating Championship game in which the advantage swung to and fro throughout the whole of the three days. The fact that the margin of runs covering the four innings was only 29 showed how close the two sides were matched on this particular occasion.

John Hampshire, who was leading the side in the absence of Boycott, decided to bat on winning the toss. He may have wished he had not done so, however, as Yorkshire were soon 17 for 3, he himself being one of the victims. Jim Love, who danced down the wicket to Titmus in only his tenth Championship innings, with some clean driving, and Peter Squires, better known as an England rugby union international winger, led a rescue act. They put together a 98-run partnership – the highest of the match – before both fell to the left-arm spin of Phil Edmonds. Love had unleashed a 'stream of thrilling strokes all round the wicket', his innings including 14 fours. Wickets then fell at regular intervals as the game swung back Middlesex's way, six batsmen being dismissed while the score increased by only 68 runs.

It was left to the less frequently needed batting skills of Geoff Cope and Steve Oldham to give the Yorkshire total some semblance of respectability. Their tenth-wicket stand of 45 gave the home team some hope of the final total of 228 being competitive enough on a pitch that was giving help to the bowlers.

Although Oldham struck early by removing Middlesex's captain Mike Brearley, two other 'Mikes', Smith and Gatting, took the visitors to a promising 98 for 1. It was

Geoff Cope – 11 for 167 in Yorkshire's narrow triumph.

then that the game took another twist as off-spinner Cope took three wickets in seven balls for the addition of only three runs. Tim Lamb, sent in as nightwatchman, stood by helplessly as two wickets, including Graham Barlow first ball, fell at the other end. The day ended with Middlesex on 101 for 4.

The second day began with the visitors' innings being rebuilt around the efforts of Norman Featherstone. Cope, bowling from the football end, was turning the ball enough to beat the bat and left-arm spinner Mike Bore also got in on the act to take his first Championship wickets for two years. The consequence was that Middlesex were gradually wheeled out and Yorkshire had a 22-run first-innings lead. Cope finished with six wickets, five of these being amongst the top seven in the order. Sadly for Middlesex, Clive Radley had been unable to bat having broken a finger when dropping a slip catch.

Richard Lumb, after having started brightly with 4 fours, was another to join the casualty list when the home side batted again and Love soon miscued and offered a simple return catch. Hampshire then compiled a very useful half-century, with Squires playing another vital supporting role. It was the turn of the Middlesex spinners to find the pitch helpful but Squires drove Titmus for two powerful on-side sixes, and play, which had been truncated by two hours lost to rain and bad light, ended four minutes early as a thunderstorm developed with Yorkshire on 110 for 2.

On the final morning, the total was taken to 133 for 2 but this compelling match turned yet again. Allan Jones, a fast bowler in his first season with Middlesex after ten years with Sussex and Somerset, broke through

Mike Bore – four top-order second-innings wickets in Yorkshire's one-run victory.

the middle-order and three wickets fell for the addition of only 14 runs. With Arnie Sidebottom (current career average 13.75) batting at no.6, Yorkshire had not wanted to have to rely on their tail-enders yet again.

Howard Cooper was the main rescuer in the latter part of this second knock and he managed to steer the home side into a position whereby Middlesex would need to make the highest score of the match – 237 – to obtain victory. This was despite the efforts of Featherstone, who produced his best Championship analysis, with his little-used off-spin, out-bowling that of the more experienced Titmus.

Once again, as it had done in all three innings thus far, the match continued to twist and turn. At 89 for 1 and again at 154 for 4, Middlesex were well placed. A good stand by Brearley and Gatting set the visitors on their way but it was Featherstone, with the highest score of the match, who again held the lower order together. The wicket continued to offer encouragement to Yorkshire's spinners but at 230 for 7 Featherstone was still at the crease and the home side looked doomed. Two

YORKSHIRE v. MIDDLESEX

wickets for two runs from the persevering Cope meant that five runs were then needed and Radley, who had been called back from London and with his arm in a sling, just had to bat. He faced up to Bore one-handed in a left-handed stance but after one ball he threw off the sling and settled into his normal stance. He cut his third ball towards the boundary but it was saved just a few feet in and the batsmen ran three. A four would have brought the scores level but Radley had kept the strike. After playing four balls safely, he was deceived by Cope at precisely three minutes to six and the joyous Bairstow completed a stumping to end his brave, but brief, resistance in a conclusion of high drama. Yorkshire had won a thrilling match by one run.

Cope ended the match with figures of 11 for 167 and, despite concern over his action, would be chosen for his first England tour to India in the following winter. As for Middlesex, they had the last laugh over Yorkshire as, in due course, the 1976 season would give them their first outright Championship for twenty-nine years. Moreover, thanks to Kerry Packer and his dispute over broadcasting rights with the Australian Cricket Board, and its far-reaching international consequences, Brearley would assume a successful leadership of his country the following season, by regaining the Ashes. Yorkshire, meanwhile, fell from what would be their highest position of the 1970s – being runners-up in 1975 – to eighth. However, this victory promised much for some of the individuals of the young side that fulfilled it.

Yorkshire's David Bairstow, keeping here to Middlesex captain Mike Brearley in 1979, made the vital stumping of Clive Radley off Cope's bowling.

YORKSHIRE v. MIDDLESEX

YORKSHIRE v. MIDDLESEX

Yorkshire won the toss and elected to bat

Umpires: W.E. Phillipson and B.J. Meyer

YORKSHIRE

R.G. Lumb	c Gould b Lamb	0	retired hurt	17
C.W.J. Athey	c Edmonds b Jones	6	c Gatting b Titmus	24
J.D. Love	c Gatting b Edmonds	77	c&b Edmonds	2
J.H. Hampshire*	lbw b Jones	0	c Brearley b Jones	59
P.J. Squires	st Gould b Edmonds	30	c Gould b Jones	30
A. Sidebottom	b Titmus	23	c sub b Jones	1
D.L. Bairstow+	lbw b Jones	2	lbw b Featherstone	13
H.P. Cooper	b Edmonds	17	c Gatting b Titmus	29
M.K. Bore	lbw b Jones	6	c&b Featherstone	14
G.A. Cope	not out	26	c Lamb b Featherstone	6
S. Oldham	c Gatting b Featherstone	19	not out	1
Extras	(b11 lb6 w1 nb4)	22	(b8 lb9 nb1)	18
TOTAL		228		214

FOW 1st: 1, 12, 17, 115, 143, 150, 167, 173, 183, 228
FOW 2nd: 35, 58, 133, 146, 147, 184, 194, 210, 214

Bowling 1st: Jones 20-6-56-4 Lamb 8-1-34-1 Titmus 24-10-46-1 Edmonds 30-13-51-3
Gatting 2-0-5-0 Featherstone 3.5-0-14-1

Bowling 2nd: Jones 16-4-44-3 Lamb 2-0-14-0 Edmonds 27-10-60-1 Titmus 21-5-66-2
Featherstone 6.4-2-12-3

MIDDLESEX

M.J. Smith	b Cope	48	c sub b Oldham	2
J.M. Brearley*	c Bairstow b Oldham	6	c Athey b Bore	44
M.W. Gatting	c Athey b Cope	38	(5) c Oldham b Bore	40
T.M. Lamb	c Lumb b Cope	15	(9) c Bairstow b Bore	6
G.D. Barlow	lbw b Cope	0	(4) c Oldham b Bore	7
N.G. Featherstone	c Squires b Bore	41	(3) c Hampshire b Cope	78
I.J. Gould+	c Cooper b Cope	14	c Athey b Cope	13
P.H. Edmonds	not out	28	(6) c sub b Cope	0
F.J. Titmus	c Hampshire b Bore	2	(8) c Bairstow b Cope	20
A.A. Jones	b Cope	0	not out	0
C.T. Radley	absent hurt		st Bairstow b Cope	3
Extras	(b1 lb2 nb11)	14	(b12 w7 nb3)	22
TOTAL		206		235

FOW 1st: 20, 98, 101, 101, 124, 162, 189, 192, 206
FOW 2nd: 12, 89, 126, 154, 158, 194, 210, 230, 232, 235

Bowling 1st: Cooper 16-1-45-0 Oldham 14-2-44-1 Bore 15-8-37-2 Cope 24.2-8-60-6 Sidebottom 2-0-6-0

Bowling 2nd: Cooper 5-1-18-0 Oldham 2-0-5-1 Cope 32.5-7-107-5 Bore 33-10-83-4

YORKSHIRE WON BY ONE RUN

WARWICKSHIRE v. YORKSHIRE

Date: 19, 20, 21 May 1982   County Championship

Location: Edgbaston

Yorkshire's tenth-wicket partnership record in first-class cricket had stood at 148 (between Lord Hawke and David Hunter against Kent) since 1898 when, on 20 May 1982, no.11 batsman Graham Stevenson, a strongly built all-rounder from Ackworth, joined Geoffrey Boycott at the wicket in the county's first innings of their Schweppes County Championship match at Edgbaston.

On a slow-seaming pitch with some inconsistent bounce, Warwickshire had been dismissed for 158 in their first innings with no one passing 40. Stevenson and Yorkshire captain Chris Old were the chief wicket-takers with three apiece. An hour before lunch on the second day, however, Warwickshire were well on top and on course to take a small, but possibly decisive, first-innings lead. Bob Willis and, in particular, Gladstone Small had reduced the visitors to 108 for 8, with opening batsman Boycott looking certain to carry his bat and only 'tailenders' Old and Stevenson to dismiss. Old, who was to join Warwickshire the following season, struck 27 out of the 35 runs added for the ninth wicket before becoming Small's seventh wicket of the innings. Yorkshire were 143 for 9. Boycott, having relished the conditions, had batted for over three hours for his 50 not out. Very quickly, as Jack Bannister recorded in his report for the *Birmingham Post* 'the improbable took shape'. Stevenson struck Willis a blow on his bowling hand as the England quick man tried to stop a thunderous drive and he found difficulty gripping the ball thereafter, and with Small tired after his successful but long spell, the remaining Warwickshire bowlers were put to the sword by the stocky no.11. In just over an hour before lunch he reached 50. He was particularly severe on the fast-medium bowling of Willie Hogg. His seven overs went for 41 runs.

After the break, Stevenson sped on past Boycott in the 70s to reach his second first-class hundred. It seemed almost inconceivable that Boycott, having batted for 340 minutes, would be the wicket that ended the partnership, but aiming to sweep the gentle leg-spin of Asif Din he was bowled for a masterly 79. The partnership had yielded 149 runs (Rob Brooke in *The Cricketer* magazine pointed out that this was the highest tenth-wicket stand involving either side and the best ever at Edgbaston) and Stevenson's 115 (his highest first-class score) had lasted 130 minutes and included 3 sixes and 15 fours. The statistical milestones were numerous: Stevenson's century was the ninth by a no.11 in all first-class cricket,

Graham Stevenson – his century was the first instance of a no.11 making a hundred in the Championship since 1947.

WARWICKSHIRE v. YORKSHIRE

the third in the County Championship, the first since Peter Smith's 163 for Essex in 1947, and before him, 112 not out by Arthur Fielder for Kent in 1909. Perhaps, above all else, his partnership with Boycott gave his side a priceless 134-run lead, which Old (6 for 76) fully exploited in Warwickshire's second innings. Only Amiss, with 75, kept the Yorkshire seam attack of Old plus Stevenson and Sidebottom at bay. Boycott saw Yorkshire home to an historic nine-wicket victory before lunch on the third morning and in doing so ensured, this time, that he was unbeaten at the end. His partnership with the likeable Stevenson turned a probable defeat into a spectacular victory in the blink of an eye.

WARWICKSHIRE v. YORKSHIRE

Yorkshire won the toss and elected to field

Umpires: R. Julian and M.J. Kitchen

WARWICKSHIRE

D.L. Amiss	c Bairstow b Stevenson	39	c Boycott b Old	75
T.A. Lloyd	b Stevenson	12	b Old	5
A.I. Kallicharran	b Sidebottom	11	c Bairstow b Sidebottom	8
G.W. Humpage+	b Boycott	4	c Sidebottom b Old	18
P.R. Oliver	c Hartley b Boycott	16	b Stevenson	9
Asif Din	c Athey b Old	13	c Boycott b Old	5
P.A. Smith	c Bairstow b Old	15	c Boycott b Sidebottom	16
G.C. Small	b Old	22	(9) c Bairstow b Old	5
R.G.D. Willis*	b Stevenson	12	(10) not out	2
J. Cumbes	c Lumb b Sidebottom	4	(8) c Sharp b Old	0
W. Hogg	not out	0	c Bairstow b Sidebottom	8
Extras	(b2 lb3 w1 nb4)	10	(lb5 w2 nb8)	15
TOTAL		158		166

FOW 1st: 21, 43, 58, 87, 92, 114, 121, 148, 158, 158
FOW 2nd: 7, 21, 50, 77, 94, 148, 148, 152, 156, 166

Bowling 1st: Old 20-7-52-3 Stevenson 18-5-41-3 Sidebottom 15.1-4-30-2 Boycott 6-1-15-2 Carrick 5-1-10-0

Bowling 2nd: Old 27-8-76-6 Sidebottom 21.3-7-34-3 Boycott 4-0-10-0 Stevenson 9-2-30-1 Carrick 2-1-1-0

YORKSHIRE

G. Boycott	b Asif Din	79	not out	21
R.G. Lumb	lbw b Small	1	lbw b Small	4
C.W.J. Athey	lbw b Small	0	not out	5
K. Sharp	c Smith b Willis	0		
S.N. Hartley	c Amiss b Willis	7		
D.L. Bairstow+	c Humpage b Small	30		
P. Carrick	lbw b Small	0		
J.P. Whiteley	c Humpage b Small	1		
A. Sidebottom	c Humpage b Small	13		
C.M. Old*	b Small	27		
G.B. Stevenson	not out	115		
Extras	(b5 lb4 w7 nb3)	19	(lb2 nb1)	3
TOTAL		292	(1 wkt)	33

FOW 1st: 2, 2, 9, 35, 89, 89, 91, 108, 143, 292
FOW 2nd: 26

Bowling 1st: Willis 23-4-71-2 Small 29-7-68-7 Hogg 7-0-41-0 Cumbes 20-8-34-0 Asif Din 12-4-27-1 Smith 5-0-32-0

Bowling 2nd: Willis 2-0-3-0 Small 7-0-13-1 Hogg 6.3-2-14-0

YORKSHIRE WON BY NINE WICKETS

NORTHAMPTONSHIRE v. YORKSHIRE

Date: 11 July 1987   Benson & Hedges Cup final
Location: Lord's

The two sides that contested the sixteenth Benson & Hedges Cup final were, at the time, the top two sides in the County Championship. A beautiful summer's day and a see-saw match that ended in the closest manner possible ensured that the game lived up to its billing. With the departure of Geoffrey Boycott and a new captain in Phil Carrick, Yorkshire had turned over a new leaf and had begun the season with seven consecutive wins in all competitions.

The two sides' recent form was very similar, both winning three and losing one of their last four limited-overs matches. In the Benson & Hedges Cup itself, Yorkshire had the superior record. They had won all four of their group matches (Northamptonshire winning only two) before very convincing wins over Hampshire by nine wickets in the quarter-final and Surrey by 76 runs in the semi-final. Northamptonshire's last two games before the final involved a 29-run win over Somerset and a five-wicket win – with only two balls to spare – against Kent.

The two teams had recently met in the Championship, in a game that had ended just eleven days previously. Despite being bowled out for 187 in their first innings, Yorkshire managed to set up a formidable run-chase on the final afternoon. The result was a session of brilliant stroke-play, the last 208 runs coming in only 27.3 overs, and Northamptonshire reaching a target of 283 for the loss of only three wickets, but with nine balls to spare.

It was felt, therefore, that the midland county, who included a top five of past, present or future England players, could well overhaul any total that Yorkshire would set. Carrick, on winning the toss, had no hesitation in inserting the opposition. Paul Jarvis set the tempo with a hostile spell and soon dismissed Geoff Cook, Northamptonshire's skipper, with a rearing delivery aimed towards his body in his second over. A swirling catch from a top edge later removed Wayne Larkins and when Martyn Moxon took a brilliant diving slip catch to send the threatening Rob Bailey on his way the score stood at 48 for 3.

Allan Lamb and David Capel then proceeded to repair the damage but when Lamb bottom-edged a catch to the 'keeper, Yorkshire knew that the main threats had gone. Or so they thought. Capel had played in the game with a heavily plastered hand and against medical advice but he proceeded to unleash some powerful drives. The Midlanders lunched on 128 for 4 after 36 overs and only Carrick, with his bowling analysis reading 8-2-18-0, had been able to stem the flow.

The afternoon session saw Capel continue on his way, ably supported by Richard Williams, who had assisted

Geoff Cook is caught by Blakey for one off the bowling of Paul Jarvis.

in grafting Northamptonshire back into the game. Stuart Fletcher conceded 22 runs from one over and the pair produced the highest fifth-wicket stand in a Lord's final. They were not parted until the fiftieth over, courtesy of Jarvis's final penetrative spell. He had always been the most threatening of Yorkshire's bowlers and each of his three previous spells had produced wickets at crucial stages in the innings. Capel perished in attempting an ambitious stroke just three runs short of a well-deserved century and, despite losing the last three wickets for 20 runs, the innings concluded as a challenging total. It was the second-highest first-innings score in the history of these finals.

Moxon and Metcalfe came into the game as Yorkshire's leading scorers in the season's competition by some distance. In fact, Metcalfe had already won four Gold Awards, creating a competition record that stood for eleven years. However, Moxon started more confidently, his partner 'caught' off a no-ball in the third over, and reached 18 before Metcalfe had even broken his duck. Thereafter, the pair benefited from some waywardness in the Northamptonshire attack. Winston Davis gave away five no-balls in his first five overs and Capel was erratic in both line and length.

After 20 overs the score had reached 83 and Cook opted for a double spin attack in Nick Cook and Williams. The ploy worked as 97 for no wicket soon became 103 for 3. Moxon was the first to perish being bowled between bat and pad, but Metcalfe and the twenty-year-old Richard Blakey both holed out to deep mid-wicket. The game had clearly swung Northamptonshire's way and Kevin Sharp and Jim Love began a rescue act that took Yorkshire to 119 for 3 at tea. This meant that with 20 overs remaining to be bowled, the required run-rate over was 6.3.

The necessary acceleration was delayed by tight bowling from Davis and Williams and the rate worryingly crept up to seven an over after a spell of 19 overs, begun before tea, which did not contain a single boundary. Love attacked Williams in his last over but the bowler replied by dismissing Sharp with his final delivery. Williams' three wickets meant that he had contributed significantly with both bat and ball. A stand of 57 had brought Yorkshire back into the game but Love remained at the crease as the last specialist batsman and the game was evenly balanced once more. David Bairstow had resigned as captain at the end of 1986 but had lost none of his enthusiasm. He saw Love go past his fifty (from 68 balls) and take 11 from Capel's last over.

With only 23 required from the final four overs, Bairstow's efforts came to a cruel end as he crashed towards the crease in a vain attempt to regain his ground. Carrick kept the momentum going but was also run out and so Davis prepared to bowl the last over with five (or four if no wickets fell) needed for victory. Three singles brought the target tantalisingly close; Arnie Sidebottom hit the fifth ball to mid-on and Bailey missed

Martyn Moxon is bowled by Nick Cook for 45 in Yorkshire's run chase.

NORTHAMPTONSHIRE v. YORKSHIRE

a run out chance by a whisker. Love sensibly blocked the final ball – a yorker – and Northamptonshire were denied victory by the closest result possible. This was not only a repeat of their 1981 NatWest final experience against Derbyshire but also in a group match against the same opponents earlier in 1987. They were due again at Lord's in 1987 for the NatWest final but lost again – this time to Nottinghamshire.

Mike Gatting duly presented Love with the Match Award and all Yorkshire fans believed that a corner in their recent history had been turned. Despite winning the John Player League in 1983, the county had finished bottom of the Championship in the same season and had won nothing since 1969. A new captain

The final ball is safely survived and Yorkshire's Arnie Sidebottom and Jim Love celebrate the Benson & Hedges Cup win by virtue of having lost fewer wickets with the scores tied.

Man of the Match Jim Love (75 not out off 93 balls) receives his Gold Award from Mike Gatting.

NORTHAMPTONSHIRE v. YORKSHIRE

and a young side should continue to deliver. In the following month, Blakey would become Yorkshire's youngest-ever double-century-maker and conclude the Championship campaign as his county's leading batsman in terms of both average and aggregate. Jarvis would make his Test debut in the following winter and Moxon would head England's batting in the same series against New Zealand.

However, that was all for the future, and the lasting impression from the day was the exultant Carrick holding the trophy aloft, with Lord's still bathed in glorious sunshine having staged and enjoyed a thrillingly dramatic match.

NORTHAMPTONSHIRE v. YORKSHIRE

Yorkshire won the toss and elected to field

Umpires: H.D. Bird and K.E. Palmer

NORTHAMPTONSHIRE

G. Cook*	c Blakey b Jarvis	1
W. Larkins	c Carrick b Hartley	15
R.J. Bailey	c Moxon b Fletcher	26
A.J. Lamb	c Bairstow b Jarvis	28
D.J. Capel	b Hartley	97
R.G. Williams	c Bairstow b Jarvis	44
D.J. Wild	b Jarvis	6
W.W. Davis	not out	10
D. Ripley+	not out	6
N.G.B. Cook		
A. Walker		
Extras	(b2 lb3 w2 nb4)	11
TOTAL	(7 wkts, 55 overs)	244

FOW: 3, 31, 48, 92, 212, 226, 232

Bowling: Jarvis 11-2-43-4 Sidebottom 11-1-40-0 Fletcher 11-1-60-1 Hartley 11-0-66-2 Carrick 11-2-30-0

YORKSHIRE

M.D. Moxon	b Cook	45
A.A. Metcalfe	c Davis b Williams	47
R.J. Blakey	c Davis b Williams	1
K. Sharp	b Williams	24
J.D. Love	not out	75
D.L. Bairstow+	run out	24
P. Carrick*	run out	10
A. Sidebottom	not out	2
P.J. Hartley		
P.W. Jarvis		
S.D. Fletcher		
Extras	(b1 lb4 w4 nb7)	16
TOTAL	(6 wkts, 55 overs)	244

FOW: 97, 101, 103, 160, 223, 235

Bowling: Davis 11-1-37-0 Walker 11-0-62-0 Capel 11-0-66-0 Cook 11-1-42-1 Williams 11-0-32-3

YORKSHIRE WON BY LOSING FEWER WICKETS

YORKSHIRE v. LANCASHIRE

Date: 1 August 1995   NatWest Trophy quarter-final
Location: Headingley

The 1995 season saw a change of direction in the style of Yorkshire's cricket. On no other occasion was this change in fortunes more epitomised than in this enthralling NatWest Trophy quarter-final game played on Yorkshire Day in front of a capacity crowd of almost 19,000. This volume of interest and support had surprised the authorities and many late-arriving spectators were unable to find the empty seats that were still available, unless helped by nearby members of the crowd, the stewarding being inadequate.

The portents for Yorkshire's success were not designed to inspire confidence amongst the home crowd. Yorkshire had won only four out of the last seventeen home limited-overs matches against Lancashire and the last time they had passed this stage in this competition was as long ago as 1982. Lancashire's record, with five final wins, was better than any other county and, just seventeen days previously, they had won the Benson & Hedges Cup.

The early skirmishes, however, went Yorkshire's way. Michael Atherton played a tired shot (he had rested for one day after leading England to victory in a Test against the West Indies). Successful bowler Darren Gough, returning from injury and playing against the England management's wishes, celebrated exultantly with an imitation of an aeroplane. With Mark Robinson bowling economically and Craig White claiming two quick wickets, the visitors were struggling at 47 for 4.

Neil Fairbrother was joined by Mike Watkinson and they rescued Lancashire with a stand of 70 – the highest of the match. Fairbrother produced some of the best strokes of the game but tried an ambitious shot against Paul Grayson and was well stumped. Wasim Akram was then deceived by a Michael Bevan 'chinaman' and 117 for 4 became 118 for 6. Watkinson was left to shepherd the tail but after he had succumbed to a fine catch taken on the run by White, the innings folded with more than six of the allotted 60 overs remaining.

When Yorkshire began their reply they soon found themselves up against some tight bowling and expert field placings. Both openers soon perished to the nagging accuracy of Ian Austin and this brought Bevan to the crease. The twenty-four-year-old Australian was in his first season with Yorkshire and had already made a considerable impact with his aggressive approach. He shared a stand of 37 with David Byas, who was captaining Yorkshire in the absence of the injured Martyn Moxon.

Meanwhile, Lancashire's spinners began to peg Yorkshire back and two quick dismissals took Yorkshire to 69 for 4 at tea. Ashley Metcalfe joined Bevan and the pair posted a half-century stand with the former providing the necessary acceleration. Yet

Yorkshire's new overseas signing Australian Michael Bevan played the pivotal innings – 60 not out – to guide the county home with three balls to spare.

another collapse (a feature of this fascinating contest) took Yorkshire to a perilous 132 for 7, still 38 runs short of victory. More importantly, many spectators were concerned that Yorkshire were well behind the run-rate. Bevan was providing the ideal stability but his progress seemed too slow.

Gough played aggressively for a while but when he departed, playing an unwise shot to Austin, 15 were still required with two wickets left. It was at this point that Bevan took the bull by the horns and hit ten from one over by Chapple. In an atmosphere of indescribable tension, Peter Hartley pulled the third ball of the last over through mid-wicket for two and Yorkshire had won a gripping contest.

Bevan deservedly gained the Man of the Match award. He had timed his 126-ball, 176-minute innings to perfection. In due course he would become regarded as the best one-day batsman in the world of his type. That type came to be known as the 'finisher', and it was a county match that witnessed one of its earliest, outstanding examples.

YORKSHIRE v. LANCASHIRE

Lancashire won the toss and elected to bat

Umpires: B. Duddleston and D.R. Shepherd

LANCASHIRE

M.A. Atherton	c Blakey b Gough	5
J.E.R. Gallian	lbw b Robinson	7
J.P. Crawley	lbw b White	13
N.H. Fairbrother	st Blakey b Grayson	46
G.D. Lloyd	c Blakey b White	0
M. Watkinson*	c White b Robinson	55
Wasim Akram	c Byas b Bevan	0
W.K. Hegg+	c Blakey b Hartley	7
I.D. Austin	not out	15
G .Yates	run out (Bevan/Blakey)	9
G. Chapple	lbw b Robinson	0
Extras	(lb2 w2 nb8)	12
TOTAL	(53.3 overs)	169

FOW: 8, 14, 47, 47, 117, 118, 136, 149, 169, 169

Bowling: Gough 9-2-18-1 Hartley 12-0-50-1 Robinson 10.3-2-21-3 White 9-0-28-2 Grayson 9-0-36-1 Bevan 4-0-14-1

YORKSHIRE

S.A. Kellett	c Hegg b Austin	6
M.P. Vaughan	c Fairbrother b Austin	14
D. Byas*	c Hegg b Yates	31
M.G. Bevan	not out	60
C. White	c Crawley b Watkinson	0
A.A. Metcalfe	c Fairbrother b Watkinson	33
R.J. Blakey+	run out (Crawley)	1
A.P. Grayson	c Hegg b Chapple	7
D. Gough	b Austin	10
P.J. Hartley	not out	3
M.A. Robinson		
Extras	(w3 nb2)	5
TOTAL	(8 wkts, 59.3 overs)	170

FOW: 20, 29, 66, 69, 121, 123, 132, 155

Bowling: Wasim 12-1-38-0 Chapple 11.3-1-47-1 Austin 12-2-32-3 Watkinson 12-0-36-2 Yates 12-2-17-1

YORKSHIRE WON BY TWO WICKETS

YORKSHIRE v. LANCASHIRE

Date: 11, 12 June 1996   Benson & Hedges Cup semi-final
Location: Old Trafford

There have been many epic Roses' encounters over the years in the longer format of the game but *Wisden Cricketers Almanack* was moved to describe the 1996 Benson & Hedges semi-final at Old Trafford as 'not only one of the great modern Roses' matches but as a contender for any list of best-ever limited-overs matches.' The game had it all – drama, excitement, highs and lows (on both sides), fluctuating fortunes and a thrilling last-ball finish.

After a long delay for rain, play finally got underway at 4.30p.m. and having lost the toss, Yorkshire were asked to bat first on a pitch that had obviously sweated under the covers throughout that damp Tuesday morning and afternoon. The Lancashire seamers exploited the favourable bowling conditions after Yorkshire slid from 66 for 1 to 83 for 5 in poor light. Michael Bevan and Richard Blakey, who was dropped on seven, started the repair work. Bevan, Yorkshire's most effective overseas signing to that point, raced to 50 in 54 balls. Following a stoppage for bad light, play resumed at 7.00p.m. and both players continued to force the pace. Blakey reached his 50 in the last over possible in the day (the forty-sixth), which cost Peter Martin 15 runs. Yorkshire closed on 198 for 5. On the Wednesday morning, a stunning 52 runs were added in the four remaining overs as the two Yorkshire batsmen raised their partnership from 115 to 167 (a sixth-wicket record for the Benson & Hedges Cup). Bevan's 95 came from 75 balls and Blakey was also unbeaten with 80 off 94 balls.

Like Yorkshire, Lancashire lost early wickets in front of the 10,000 spectators that had gathered for day two of this enthralling contest. Mike Atherton edged one to David Byas at slip in Darren Gough's first over and the paceman sent the England skipper on his way in the heat of battle. Chris Silverwood removed South African Steve Elworthy and Mike Watkinson was run out. Lancashire were 48 for 3 after 15 overs. When Nick Speak and Graham Lloyd both departed, Lancashire needed a further 154 with only five wickets in hand at over seven runs per over. Neil Fairbrother and Warren Hegg shared the first substantial partnership (64) for the home side before Fairbrother became the third run-out victim of the innings. When Ian Austin went cheaply, Lancashire still needed 90 runs for victory in the 10 remaining overs. Hegg dispatched White for 2 sixes and in an extraordinary display of hitting (mixed with good fortune) reduced the target to 11 from 13 balls before White clean bowled him.

The Lancashire wicketkeeper made 81 off just 62 balls, a display that ultimately won him the Gold Award. The penultimate over, bowled by Gough,

Richard Blakey – 80 not out off 94 balls – in a new tournament sixth-wicket record partnership with Bevan of 167 in this thrilling Roses clash.

YORKSHIRE v. LANCASHIRE

cost only three runs and Yates was run out leaving eight runs required from White's last over with the final pair (Glen Chapple and Martin) together. Chapple hit the first ball for four; a wide and a single followed before Martin missed the fourth and fifth. However, he hit the final ball to deep cover, beat Michael Vaughan's desperate return to the wicket, and in the process collected the two runs that took Lancashire through to the final (for the fifth time in seven years) and left Yorkshire's players and supporters desolate in defeat.

YORKSHIRE v. LANCASHIRE

Lancashire won the toss and elected to field

Umpires: D.J. Constant and K.E. Palmer

YORKSHIRE

D. Byas*	c Hegg b Martin	22
M.D. Moxon	c Atherton b Watkinson	25
M.P. Vaughan	c Atherton b Chapple	15
M.G. Bevan	not out	95
A. McGrath	c Hegg b Elworthy	0
C. White	c Hegg b Watkinson	4
R.J. Blakey+	not out	80
P.J. Hartley		
D. Gough		
C.E.W. Silverwood		
R.D. Stemp		
Extras	(lb6 w3)	9
TOTAL	(5 wkts, 50 overs)	250

FOW: 29, 66, 77, 78, 83

Bowling: Austin 10-0-54-0 Martin 10-0-62-1 Chapple 10-0-46-1 Elworthy 10-0-52-1 Watkinson 10-1-30-2

LANCASHIRE

M.A. Atherton	c Byas b Gough	0
M. Watkinson*	run out (Bevan)	6
N.J. Speak	run out (Vaughan/Stemp)	34
S. Elworthy	c Gough b Silverwood	12
N.H. Fairbrother	run out (White)	59
G.D. Lloyd	c Blakey b Silverwood	9
W.K. Hegg+	b White	81
I.D. Austin	c&b Gough	5
G. Yates	run out (McGrath/Blakey)	26
G. Chapple	not out	6
P.J. Martin	not out	2
Extras	(lb4 w1 nb6)	11
TOTAL	(9 wkts, 50 overs)	251

FOW: 2, 21, 36, 79, 97, 161, 174, 240, 243

Bowling: Gough 10-1-39-2 Silverwood 10-2-40-2 Hartley 10-1-47-0 White 10-1-74-1 Stemp 10-0-47-0

LANCASHIRE WON BY ONE WICKET

YORKSHIRE v. ESSEX

Date: 29, 30, 31 August, 2 September 1996   County Championship
Location: Headingley

Essex came to Headingley for their Championship match with Yorkshire as the 'form' side on the back of five successive wins in the competition, a run that had seen them rise to joint top spot in the table with only four games left to play. Under new captain David Byas, Yorkshire had challenged strongly in all competitions but two defeats, against Lancashire in the Benson & Hedges and NatWest Trophy semi-finals, were harsh blows to morale. Rain and bad weather had effectively ended their Championship push in the previous match, ironically once more against Lancashire at Leeds. Both counties went into this fixture without their influential Australian batsmen, Stuart Law (Essex) and Michael Bevan (Yorkshire), who had departed for national pre-tour training.

On a Headingley pitch offering the bowlers some assistance, Byas chose to bat first. Martyn Moxon batted with his usual skill and craft for 59 but Yorkshire were 141 for 5 before Craig White and Richard Blakey forged a recovery, adding 115 in 25 overs. Mark Ilott wrapped up the tail with three wickets at no cost before the third bonus point could be secured. Essex closed the first day on 79 for 2, which included the wicket of forty-three-year-old Graham Gooch. Nasser Hussain's disciplined and cultured innings of 158 (although missed on 98) on day two gave his side a significant 82-run lead. He added 135 with skipper Pritchard for the third wicket and 194 runs were scored by Essex before lunch against poor Yorkshire bowling and fielding. Hamilton, bowling fast and straight, limited the visitors' lead as they lost their last seven wickets for 115. With the surface offering help to bowlers of all types, the home side declined to 66 for 4 against off-break bowler Peter Such. Sheffield left-hander Richard Kettleborough (playing in Bevan's absence) and 'keeper Blakey stood firm as Yorkshire closed on 119 for 5, a slender lead of only 37. There was only a smattering of spectators present on day three in what turned into a remarkable and unexpected transformation in fortunes. Kettleborough batted in total for six hours and twenty minutes. He played straight, moved his feet well against the spin of Such and Grayson and gave no chances. He shared in two crucial partnerships – 102 with Blakey and 93 with Gavin Hamilton, who in his first Championship match of the season registered his maiden first-class fifty via

an extravagant display of hitting. Kettleborough, though, was the real hero, his 108 was his first century at that level of the game and it gave Yorkshire a total to defend against a now shattered and confidence-drained Essex. By the end of Saturday's play, Byas and his side were in command of the match as the visitors crashed from 74 for 1 to 98 for 5. When play resumed on the Monday, Yorkshire's slow left-arm bowler Richard Stemp found the sharp-turning pitch to his liking and brought the Essex resistance to a speedy conclusion with his best Championship figures (5 for 38) for two years.

This improbable victory was hailed by captain David Byas as 'the best rear guard action I've ever seen from a Yorkshire side'. By the close of the 1997 season Kettleborough had left Yorkshire for Middlesex and within two years had departed the county game altogether. Today he is pursuing a new career as a first-class umpire. The tenacious left-hander's highest first-class score will long be remembered in the modern history of Yorkshire CCC Championship cricket.

Richard Kettleborough – his maiden century transformed the game for Yorkshire.

YORKSHIRE v. ESSEX

YORKSHIRE v. ESSEX

Yorkshire won the toss and elected to bat

Umpires: J.C. Balderstone and K.J. Lyons

YORKSHIRE

Batsman	1st dismissal	1st	2nd dismissal	2nd
M.D. Moxon	c Hussain b Williams	59	b Such	23
M.P. Vaughan	c Gooch b Williams	3	lbw b Such	10
D. Byas*	c Hussain b Gooch	23	c Grayson b Such	4
A. McGrath	c Lewis b Such	16	c Lewis b Such	18
R.A. Kettleborough	b Williams	28	lbw b Such	108
C. White	c Rollins b Grayson	76	b Grayson	10
R.J. Blakey+	c Grayson b Ilott	57	c Rollins b Ilott	44
P.J. Hartley	c Prichard b Grayson	2	c Lewis b Such	20
G.M. Hamilton	not out	9	b Such	61
C.E.W. Silverwood	c Rollins b Ilott	0	c Lewis b Such	1
R.D. Stemp	c Lewis b Ilott	0	not out	1
Extras	(b4 lb9 nb4)	17	(b7 lb16 nb6)	29
TOTAL		290		329

FOW 1st: 4, 51, 99, 127, 141, 256, 264, 286, 286, 290
FOW 2nd: 18, 26, 43, 66, 91, 193, 224, 317, 326, 329

Bowling 1st: Ilott 15.1-0-63-3 Williams 15-3-52-3 Cowan 13-1-74-0 Gooch 13-5-20-1 Such 19-6-47-1 Grayson 9-4-21-2

Bowling 2nd: Ilott 13-3-43-1 Williams 19-2-44-0 Such 46.2-7-118-8 Cowan 11-1-39-0 Grayson 22-1-62-1

ESSEX

Batsman	1st dismissal	1st	2nd dismissal	2nd
G.A. Gooch	c Blakey b Hartley	15	b White	30
A.P. Grayson	c Byas b Silverwood	9	b Hartley	15
N. Hussain	b White	158	c Silverwood b Vaughan	38
P.J. Prichard*	b White	71	c Kettleborough b Stemp	2
J.J.B. Lewis	lbw b Hamilton	33	run out (Kettleborough/Moxon)	2
S.D. Peters	c Blakey b Vaughan	0	lbw b Stemp	11
R.J. Rollins+	c Byas b Stemp	18	(8) c White b Vaughan	23
M.C. Ilott	c Blakey b Hamilton	26	(9) lbw b Stemp	6
N.F. Williams	c White b Hamilton	15	(10) c Hamilton b Stemp	1
A.P. Cowan	b White	0	(11) not out	0
P.M. Such	not out	0	(7) c Byas b Stemp	0
Extras	(b8 lb5 nb14)	27	(b9 lb4 nb8)	21
TOTAL		372		149

FOW 1st: 19, 54, 189, 257, 264, 300, 342, 367, 372, 372
FOW 2nd: 39, 74, 81, 84, 98, 100, 131, 143, 146, 149

Bowling 1st: Silverwood 12-1-60-1 Hamilton 19.4-1-65-3 Hartley 19-2-73-1 White 15-0-45-3 Stemp 13-1-60-1 Vaughan 8-0-56-1

Bowling 2nd: Silverwood 5-0-17-0 Hamilton 6-0-14-0 Hartley 8-1-20-1 Stemp 24-7-38-5 White 9-0-33-1 Vaughan 8-1-14-2

YORKSHIRE WON BY 98 RUNS

Gavin Hamilton (batting here for Scotland in the 1999 World Cup) – in his first Championship appearance of the season – scored 61 and shared an eighth-wicket stand of 93 with Kettleborough.

YORKSHIRE v. LANCASHIRE

Date: 27, 28, 29, 30 July 2001   County Championship

Location: Headingley

With glorious sunshine throughout all four days, this magnificent match epitomised the glory of four-day Championship cricket at its very best. Played on an excellent pitch, the crowd witnessed one of the finest individual innings ever played on the historic ground. Yorkshire came into the game as leaders in the Championship race. Although Somerset were in second place, it was regarded that the most vital remaining games would be two against each of Lancashire and Surrey. The Red Rose county had begun the 2001 campaign well with four wins in their first seven games but had since faded somewhat, losing both of their two most recent fixtures. Yorkshire, meanwhile, had not lost since the second game of the season and had won four of their last six games.

But for a late flurry of wickets, Darren Gough snaring three victims in four balls, day one would have belonged to Lancashire. The visitors won the toss but had to recover twice from slightly parlous situations. Steve Kirby achieved some early bounce in taking the first two wickets but much of the bowling lacked the necessary accuracy. Joe Scuderi raced to a 51-ball half-century but he holed out to deep square leg and an obvious plan. Skipper John Crawley held the innings together for a time but the real rescue act came from Warren Hegg and Chris Schofield as they compiled a sixth-wicket stand of 115. As the day neared its end with the Red Rose county on 348 for 6, many Yorkshire supporters began to fear what had become, over the previous six seasons, an annual late-campaign demise. However, Gough had other ideas and dismissed Hegg and Peter Martin with successive deliveries before disposing of Glen Chapple.

Resuming on 358 for 9 at the start of the second day, Lancashire added a further 15 runs before Kirby claimed his third victim. Craig White, whose bowling had disappointed the watching England coach Duncan Fletcher on the previous day, was promoted to open the innings but fared little better. Anthony McGrath soon followed him back to the pavilion but, for the remainder of the day, the Saturday crowd of over 3,000 was treated to a batting masterclass of supreme quality from Darren Lehmann. Even most of his partners were left looking inadequate as he reduced each of the bowlers, even the persevering Chapple, to mere proverbial cannon-fodder.

Matthew Wood took part in a stand of 169 with Lehmann but he was the only partner not to be completely put in the shade. David Byas, for example, contributed just seven to a stand of 61 (in 13 overs) and Richard Blakey 18 out of 86. Lehmann announced his presence with a pre-lunch leg-side six off the left-arm spin of Yorkshire-born Gary Keedy and the same bowler suffered again just before tea

Fast bowler Steve Kirby made an immediate impact following his mid-season signing from Leicestershire. He dismissed the England and Lancashire opening batsman Mike Atherton in both innings of the Leeds match.

YORKSHIRE v. LANCASHIRE

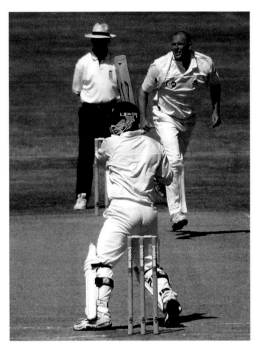

Darren Lehmann cuts a ball away off the bowling of John Wood during his first innings' 252 – he made 300 runs in the match and passed 1,000 runs for the season.

as a drive through extra cover brought the Australian his century. In the final session, Lehmann took advantage of a wilting attack and his score from 110 to 222 with a majestic blend of timing and power. His second century took just 86 balls.

The third day began with the home side on 376 for 5. Blakey and Richard Dawson both fell but Gough came out to play a brash and entertaining knock. He dominated a half-century stand with Lehmann; this ended with the latter being bowled middle-stump by the persevering Chapple for the highest individual score ever made in a Roses match. He had faced 288 balls and hit 1 six and 35 fours. With two wickets remaining, Yorkshire already had a first-innings lead of 74 and the match was interestingly poised.

Although Ryan Sidebottom did not last long, Gough found a more than capable tenth-wicket partner in Kirby. Gough reached 50 from a mere 34 balls – his first half-century in 68 innings – swept Schofield in both directions but eventually chased a wide one from Andrew Flintoff falling just four runs short of what would have been his second first-class century. With the watchful Kirby surviving for 67 balls (one of them being a no-ball hooked for six) he had added 83 and taken Yorkshire's first-innings lead to 158.

The exultant Kirby removed Michael Atherton cheaply for the second time in the match and with the score on 3 for 2 Crawley began to play his second fine innings of the game. Support was minimal this time round, however, and Lancashire lost five wickets before wiping off the deficit. Despite this, Crawley continued to attack fluently taking 3 fours from Dawson's first over and hitting a six over wide long-on. Byas, having taken two good catches at slip, showed his frustration as the excited Gough constantly pitched too short, Crawley hitting him for 3 fours in quick succession. Wickets kept on falling, however, and Crawley eventually fell to a catch at the wicket off the bowling of the persevering White. At 233 for 8 Lancashire led by only 75 but tail-enders Martin and John Wood had other ideas and concluded the final session with some entertaining hitting. A pulsating day had produced no less than 435 runs and 13 wickets and Lancashire ended on 280 for 8 – a lead of 122 runs.

The Yorkshire bowlers did not have to toil for long on the final morning, Gary Fellows helping matters with a direct hit from cover to run out John Wood and the victory target was 157. With the wicket now taking some spin, Lancashire hoped to make matters difficult for the home side but it was not to be. Wood made his second half-century of the game with some stylish strokeplay and when his wicket was the second to fall, half the target had already disappeared. Keedy was producing some turn and took all three wickets that eventually fell but Lehmann hit him for 2 sixes and showed scant respect in racing to 48 and

YORKSHIRE v. LANCASHIRE

a score that gave him exactly 300 runs for the match. He was out when only 13 runs were required for victory and Byas hit 3 fours in Keedy's next over to conclude what had been a wonderful game.

The result of this match meant that Yorkshire had defeated Lancashire in the Championship for the first time since 1995 and at Headingley for the first time in nine years. The 1,376 runs scored created a new record for a match aggregate in a Championship game at Headingley. Yorkshire drew their next fixture – against Surrey – and then went to Old Trafford to defeat their hosts by an innings in two and a half days. (Lancashire's campaign faded so much that their last win occurred as early as 22 June and they finished just one place above the relegation zone). This gave Yorkshire their first Roses double since 1987 and, with most of their rivals being held up by the weather, meant that a maximum of 36 points from four matches would secure the title for the first time since 1968.

This proved to be more of a formality than even the most optimistic Tyke could hope for and the title was won, against Glamorgan at Scarborough on 24 August, with two games remaining. All those who followed the exhilarating 2001 season, however, knew that Lehmann's magnificent innings and a four-day sunlit Headingley in late July provided a huge impetus for the campaign's final month and its much-welcomed success.

Lehmann celebrates reaching his double-century.

YORKSHIRE v. LANCASHIRE

Lancashire won the toss and elected to bat

Umpires: B. Dudleston and J.W. Lloyds

LANCASHIRE

M.A. Atherton	c Wood b Kirby	17	c Byas b Kirby	1
M.J. Chilton	b Kirby	0	lbw b Gough	2
J.P. Crawley*	c&b Dawson	73	c Blakey b White	113
A. Flintoff	c Byas b Sidebottom	12	c Byas b White	21
J.C. Scuderi	c White b Gough	56	c Blakey b Sidebottom	7
W.K. Hegg+	c Dawson b Gough	76	c&b Dawson	14
C.P. Schofield	c Byas b Sidebottom	55	c Lehmann b Kirby	34
G. Chapple	c McGrath b Gough	33	c Byas b White	0
P.J. Martin	b Gough	0	not out	51
J. Wood	c Dawson b Kirby	12	run out (Fellows)	35
G. Keedy	not out	12	c Blakey b White	4
Extras	(b4 lb5 nb18)	27	(lb10 w6 nb16)	32
TOTAL		373		314

FOW 1st: 4, 35, 63, 138, 173, 288, 348, 348, 349, 373
FOW 2nd: 3, 3, 66, 100, 149, 203, 203, 233, 301, 314

Bowling 1st: Gough 24-4-65-4 Kirby 23.4-4-103-3 Sidebottom 16-5-45-2 White 15-2-43-0
Fellows 2-0-11-0 Dawson 18-3-62-1 Lehmann 9-1-35-0

Bowling 2nd: Gough 20-1-96-1 Kirby 12-2-48-2 Sidebottom 15-5-31-1 White 17.1-3-57-4
Dawson 11-0-62-1 Lehmann 5-3-10-0

YORKSHIRE

C. White	c Hegg b Chapple	23	b Keedy	19
M.J. Wood	c Hegg b Wood	86	c Flintoff b Keedy	51
A. McGrath	c&b Chapple	0	not out	21
D.S. Lehmann	b Chapple	252	b Keedy	48
D. Byas*	c Schofield b Flintoff	7	not out	14
G.M. Fellows	c Hegg b Martin	5		
R.J. Blakey+	c Chilton b Chapple	18		
R.K.J. Dawson	c Atherton b Chapple	0		
D. Gough	c Hegg b Flintoff	96		
R.J. Sidebottom	c Hegg b Martin	0		
S.P. Kirby	not out	15		
Extras	(b4 lb7 w4 nb14)	29	(lb1 nb4)	5
TOTAL		531	(3 wkts)	158

FOW 1st: 31, 45, 214, 275, 300, 386, 396, 447, 448, 531
FOW 2nd: 55, 80, 144

Bowling 1st: Martin 28-4-113-2 Chapple 22-7-83-5 Wood 15-0-84-1 Flintoff 18.2-3-55-2
Keedy 28-3-103-0 Schofield 22-6-67-0 Scuderi 1-0-15-0

Bowling 2nd: Martin 5-1-13-0 Chapple 4-0-23-0 Flintoff 7-1-27-0 Keedy 10.5-1-67-3 Wood 2-1-10-0
Schofield 5-3-17-0

YORKSHIRE WON BY SEVEN WICKETS

YORKSHIRE v. NOTTINGHAMSHIRE

Date: 26 August 2001   Norwich Union League

Location: Scarborough

Two days before this Norwich Union League Division One clash with the Nottinghamshire Outlaws, Yorkshire had clinched their first County Championship crown in thirty-three years following an innings victory against Glamorgan at Scarborough, and there was a real feeling of euphoria amongst the 6,000 strong crowd at the North Marine Road ground.

Entering this match the prospect of relegation in the 45-over competition was a real possibility for the orange and black clad Yorkshire Phoenix. Victory over the Outlaws would provide four vital points towards Division One survival as well as the 'double' over the Nottinghamshire visitors. What followed, on that dry but overcast Sunday afternoon on the East coast, was a remarkable display of 'beautiful violence', as the *Yorkshire Post* cricket correspondent Robert Mills later described it, by Yorkshire's Australian colossus Darren Lehmann.

Put into bat by the Outlaws, Gavin Hamilton and Matthew Wood set the tone for the Phoenix innings with an opening stand of 46 in the first eight overs. Hamilton (24 off 20 balls) and Wood both departed within the space of six runs and Anthony McGrath was joined by Lehmann with the score on 52 for 2. In the next 116 minutes there was total mayhem. Less than a month after notching the highest score in Roses' cricket history (252), the sturdy Aussie left-hander, described by his county captain David Byas as 'the Don Bradman of county cricket', registered Yorkshire's highest limited-overs score (beating Craig White's [his brother-in-law!] 148 in 1997 versus Leicestershire). By later standards, his first fifty came at a relatively sedate pace – 38 balls! His hundred came off 67 balls (eighty-one minutes); his third fifty took a mere 19 deliveries. McGrath contributed 38 in a third-wicket stand worth 172 in 22 pulsating overs. Lehmann went onto smash a further 62 of the 80 runs added with White in their seven-over alliance. Brilliantly caught by Clough, on the long-on boundary, off another screaming drive, Lehmann departed to a standing ovation having scored 191 off 103 balls with 20 fours and 11 sixes (three of which were hit out

Darren Lehmann turns a short ball to leg during his chanceless 191 from 103 balls at North Marine Road.

YORKSHIRE v. NOTTINGHAMSHIRE

of the ground). His innings was the highest ever made against Nottinghamshire in one-day cricket. The brutal assault had been held up only by an ambulance that was driven on to the field to attend to an ill spectator in the Trafalgar Square stand. Yorkshire's final tally of 352 for 6 was the county's highest-ever one-day total and only Surrey's Alistair Brown (203) had registered a higher League score than Lehmann.

Numb from their mauling, the Outlaw batsmen started in positive fashion but the loss of Darren Bicknell (50), Paul Johnson and Kevin Pietersen in successive overs from Hamilton restricted their charge. With Greg Blewett (Yorkshire's overseas batsman in 1999) bowled by White for 25 the game was effectively over and Nottinghamshire fell away badly to 173 all out inside of their 45 overs. To complete 'his' match, Lehmann picked up two wickets and took a catch.

Yorkshire's crushing 179-run victory over Nottinghamshire in this match certainly wasn't a tightly fought encounter but for those spectators who witnessed Lehmann's destruction that afternoon at Scarborough, the game will linger long in the memory, probably not so for the opposition bowlers!

YORKSHIRE v. NOTTINGHAMSHIRE

Nottinghamshire won the toss and elected to field

Umpires: A. Clarkson and D.J. Constant

YORKSHIRE

G.M. Hamilton	c Read b Logan	24
M.J. Wood	c Bicknell b Smith	23
A. McGrath	c Johnson b Logan	38
D.S. Lehmann	c Clough b Pietersen	191
C. White	c Clough b Pietersen	25
G.M. Fellows	not out	22
D. Byas*	c Logan b Clough	5
R.J. Blakey+	not out	8
R.K.J. Dawson		
C.J. Elstub		
M.J. Hoggard		
Extras	(b1 lb8 w7)	16
TOTAL	(6wkts, 45 overs)	352

FOW: 46, 52, 224, 304, 326, 334

Bowling: Smith 9-1-46-1 Malik 7-0-65-0 Logan 9-0-73-2 Clough 7-0-51-1 Randall 4-0-42-0 Pietersen 9-0-66-2

NOTTINGHAMSHIRE

D.J. Bicknell*	c Blakey b Hamilton	50
G.E. Welton	lbw b Elstub	20
G.S. Blewett	b White	25
P. Johnson	c Lehmann b Hamilton	2
K.P. Pietersen	c Fellows b Hamilton	5
C.M.W. Read+	c Wood b Lehmann	36
G.D. Clough	c Byas b Dawson	2
R.J. Logan	st Blakey b Lehmann	5
S.J. Randall	not out	13
G.J. Smith	b Dawson	5
M.N. Malik	b McGrath	1
Extras	(lb5 w4)	9
TOTAL	(43.3 overs)	173

FOW: 32, 95, 100, 104, 109, 116, 141, 160, 170, 173

Bowling: Hoggard 6-0-31-0 Elstub 7-1-23-1 White 7-0-28-1 Lehmann 9-0-38-2 Hamilton 5-0-14-3 Dawson 9-0-33-2 McGrath 0.3-0-1-1

YORKSHIRE WON BY 179 RUNS

YORKSHIRE v. SOMERSET

Date: 31 August 2002   Cheltenham & Gloucester Trophy final
Location: Lord's

Yorkshire entered the C&G Trophy Final against the back-drop of financial crisis at the Club, and the almost inevitable realisation that relegation from Division One of the County Championship was upon them (having won the title for the first time in thirty-three years the previous season). Led by wicket-keeper Richard Blakey – in the absence of their hugely influential overseas batsman and captain Darren Lehmann (on international duties) – the White Rose county line-up, already missing the 'adopted' South Australian, was short also of stalwarts Darren Gough and Gavin Hamilton. Injury to Craig White meant that he played as a batsman only and Chris Silverwood bowled despite a chipped bone in his foot. The tall Victorian left-handed batsman Matthew Elliott, signed by Yorkshire two-and-a-half weeks prior to the final, filled the impressive 'Lehmann void'. Somerset, equally at strife in the longer version of the game, welcomed back their England opener Marcus Trescothick, after seven weeks out with a broken left thumb, and took the field with the same eleven players who had secured the trophy the previous summer.

Trescothick got his West Country side off to a thumping start, in front of a sell out 28,000 strong crowd, following Jamie Cox's decision to bat first. He took 20 runs off his England colleague Matthew Hoggard in one over and blazed his way to 27 having been caught off a no-ball. The momentum was altered by a quite stunning catch by Michael Vaughan, who took off to his far right at short cover and held a full blooded drive to remove Trescothick. Somerset, 82 for 1 after 15 overs, seemed to lose their way mid-innings and although Peter Bowler (67), Cox (34) and Michael Burns (21) looked well set, Hoggard for Yorkshire, when not going for runs, picked up regular wickets (finishing with 5 for 65 from his 10 overs) to help restrict the reigning C&G champions to 256 for 8, probably 20 or 30 short of their initial expectations.

Richard Johnson, in an impressive opening burst, removed White and 'pinch-hitter' Silverwood in his fourth over, to reduce Yorkshire to 19 for 2. When Matthew Wood became Johnson's third victim, the Tykes were 64 for 3 in the 15th over. Enter Elliott, who joined the seemingly composed Michael Vaughan at the wicket. Together the pair added 93 for the fourth wicket in 20 overs, content to play the ball into gaps, rotate the strike and regroup. Vaughan's demise brought Anthony McGrath to the crease and the decisive, unbroken 103-run partnership with Elliott got underway. This was Elliott's first C&G outing and from the start he exerted an assured and controlling presence. The Australian Test outcast faced 120 balls for his unbeaten 128, mixing forceful driving with whipped leg-side glances, often from down the pitch. McGrath batted with purpose too and by the time Elliott struck his 16th boundary, Somerset were a beaten side (by six wickets with two overs to spare). The roar of victory from the Yorkshire followers was loud and enduring.

Blakey lifted the trophy, last won by Yorkshire when it was the Gillette Cup back in 1969. It was the county's first one-day trophy since the Benson & Hedges Cup win fifteen years earlier. The £53,000 prize money came as a welcome deposit to the Club's beleaguered coffers and, in the evening

Elliott flicks a ball off his pads during his match-winning innings of 128 from 125 balls. Somerset keeper Rob Turner is behind the wicket.

sunshine, Elliott stepped forward to pick up the Man of the Match award. Not even Lehmann could have been expected to match the deeds of his 'stand-in' fellow countryman.

YORKSHIRE v. SOMERSET

Somerset won the toss and elected to bat

Umpires: J.W. Holder and G. Sharp

SOMERSET

P.D. Bowler	c Blakey b Hoggard	67
M.E. Trescothick	c Vaughan b Hoggard	27
J. Cox*	lbw b McGrath	34
M. Burns	lbw b Hoggard	21
I.D. Blackwell	b Sidebottom	12
K.A. Parsons	c Sidebottom b Hoggard	41
R.J. Turner+	c White b Sidebottom	20
R.L. Johnson	b Hoggard	2
K.P. Dutch	not out	13
A.R. Caddick	not out	0
P.S. Jones		
Extras	(b1 lb6 w6 nb)	19
TOTAL	(8 wkts, 50 overs)	256

FOW: 41, 122, 159, 171, 191, 230, 233, 250

Bowling: Silverwood 8-1-30-0 Hoggard 10-0-65-5 Sidebottom 9-0-49-2 McGrath 9-0-37-1 Dawson 10-0-48-0 Vaughan 4-0-20-0

YORKSHIRE

C. White	c Turner b Johnson	12
M.J. Wood	b Johnson	19
C.E.W. Silverwood	b Johnson	0
M.T.G. Elliott	not out	128
M.P. Vaughan	lbw b Jones	31
A. McGrath	not out	46
G.M. Fellows		
R.J. Blakey*+		
R.K.J. Dawson		
M.J. Hoggard		
R.J. Sidebottom		
Extras	(lb7 w15 nb2)	24
TOTAL	(4 wkts, 48 overs)	260

FOW: 19, 19, 64, 157

Bowling: Caddick 9-0-53-0 Johnson 10-2-51-3 Parsons 6-0-31-0 Jones 9-0-45-1 Dutch 8-0-43-0 Blackwell 6-0-30-0

YORKSHIRE WON BY SIX WICKETS

Vice-Captain Matthew Wood with the C&G Trophy.

LEICESTERSHIRE v. YORKSHIRE

Date: 11, 12, 13, 14 May 2005   County Championship
Location: Grace Road, Leicester

This absorbing game saw Yorkshire achieving a score that broke their seventy-five-year-old record for the highest fourth innings total to win a match – the record being smashed by 75 runs. The two teams went into the game with contrasting early-season records. In all competitions Leicestershire had won only one of their last eight games, whereas the visitors were looking for a seventh consecutive win.

The game started on a flat pitch and so little effect did Yorkshire's bowlers have on the surface that off-spinner Richard Dawson bowled as early as the fifth over and five bowlers were used in the first 15 overs. Although the openers put on over 50, Tim Bresnan dismissed Darren Robinson with a delivery that reared up awkwardly and Danesh Mongia followed almost immediately for a 'golden duck'. Thereafter Yorkshire were able to take wickets at crucial times and although Hylton Ackerman played a fluent innings, none of the last six batsmen got into double figures and Matthew Hoggard took the tenth wicket – his 400th in first-class cricket – with the final ball of the day.

In the week following this match there would be the 100th anniversary of the highest individual innings ever played for Yorkshire (see page 34), coincidentally against the same opponents. However, in 2005, things were a lot different and although there was some swing for the bowlers, the pitch was still true and there was no excuse for Yorkshire losing seven wickets before lunch. The thirty-six-year-old West Indian Ottis Gibson took 4 for 9 in 21 balls, his first three victims all being caught in the wicketkeeper/slip cordon. Only Ismail Dawood showed application although Dawson managed to stay with him for a 61-run stand for the seventh wicket before the visitors were all out in 45.4 overs and conceded a first innings deficit of 127 runs. Leicestershire lost five wickets – Ian Harvey bowling skilfully but with little luck – in extending this by a further 183 runs before the close.

The third day was played in glorious sunshine and gale force winds – so severe were these that the ground-staff had to use poles to prop up the sight screens. The pitch remained excellent although a few deliveries kept low and the medium-pacers caused some problems. Despite the match situation Yorkshire bowled tidily and fielded enthusiastically. The declaration came almost immediately after lunch and Leicestershire seemed over-confident as the visitors' openers gave Yorkshire a flying start in their quest to score 404 to win. Michael Vaughan, the England captain, batted in his usual fluent and stylish manner and close of play came with Yorkshire on 261 for 3. Anthony McGrath, who had started on a king pair, was 70 not out.

As the fourth morning wore on the home side's bowling became increasingly ragged and the victory target was reached just before lunch, in an almost effortless manner, 143 runs coming in just 29.1 overs. McGrath extended his fourth-wicket partnership with Ian Harvey to 133 and hit his 20th four for the winning runs through mid-wicket. He had batted for 281 minutes and faced 218 balls in a magnificent innings in which his best strokes were 'powered with lovely timing' through the leg-side.

Anthony McGrath – 165 not out in Yorkshire's historic second innings run chase at Grace Road.

LEICESTERSHIRE v. YORKSHIRE

This result took Yorkshire to second place in the Championship Second Division table with three wins from four games. Remarkably, two months later in the return fixture at Scarborough, Leicestershire had an even bigger first-innings lead – 179 runs – but Yorkshire again scored 400 to win by the same margin of six wickets. These two victories were important factors in the White Rose county gaining promotion after just three seasons in the bottom flight.

LEICESTERSHIRE v. YORKSHIRE

Leicestershire won the toss and elected to bat

Umpires: V.A. Holder and A.G.T. Whitehead

LEICESTERSHIRE

D.D.J. Robinson	c Dawood b Bresnan	42	b Hoggard	6
D.L. Maddy	lbw b McGrath	53	lbw b Harvey	27
D. Mongia	lbw b Harvey	0	c Dawood b Dawson	70
A. Habib	b McGrath	41	lbw b Bresnan	16
H.D. Ackerman*	not out	85	c Jaques b McGrath	30
P.A. Nixon+	c Wood b Dawson	0	b Kruis	68
O.D. Gibson	lbw b Kruis	6	c Dawson b Hoggard	9
P.A.J. DeFreitas	c Dawood b Kruis	6	lbw b Harvey	17
C.W. Henderson	b Bresnan	5	c McGrath b Dawson	10
D.D. Masters	c Dawood b Kruis	8	not out	9
C.M. Willoughby	b Hoggard	2		
Extras	(lb12 nb18)	30	(lb8 nb6)	14
TOTAL		278	(9 wkts dec)	276

FOW 1st: 62, 63, 151, 170, 199, 211, 223, 239, 259, 278
FOW 2nd: 20, 66, 107, 130, 170, 188, 226, 255, 276

Bowling 1st: Hoggard 20.5-1-57-1 Kruis 20-8-40-3 Dawson 6-1-18-1 Bresnan 17-6-38-2 Harvey 13-2-61-1 McGrath 26-7-52-2

Bowling 2nd: Hoggard 16-4-53-2 Kruis 13.5-3-45-1 Bresnan 12-4-32-1 Harvey 22-5-54-2 McGrath 15-1-42-1 Dawson 12-1-42-2

YORKSHIRE

M.J. Wood	c Nixon b Gibson	17	c Nixon b Maddy	48
P.A. Jaques	c Robinson b Gibson	14	lbw b DeFreitas	37
A. McGrath	c Ackerman b Gibson	0	not out	165
M.P. Vaughan	lbw b Masters	9	b Henderson	53
I.J. Harvey	b Gibson	1	b DeFreitas	47
C. White*	c Nixon b Masters	0	not out	34
I. Dawood+	not out	62		
R.K.J. Dawson	c Robinson b Maddy	29		
T.T. Bresnan	c Nixon b Gibson	2		
M.J. Hoggard	b Gibson	2		
G.J. Kruis	c Habib b Henderson	4		
Extras	(lb6 nb4 w1)	11	(b1 lb8 nb6 w7)	22
TOTAL		151	(4 wkts)	406

FOW 1st: 27, 27, 44, 44, 45, 45, 106, 124, 134, 151
FOW 2nd: 94, 100, 184, 317

Bowling 1st: Gibson 17-3-56-6 Willoughby 8-1-18-0 Masters 8-1-28-2 DeFreitas 4-0-18-0 Maddy 2-0-6-1 Henderson 6.4-0-19-1

Bowling 2nd: Gibson 24.1-1-124-0 Willoughby 13-0-69-0 Masters 11-2-36-0 Maddy 18-2-70-1 DeFreitas 11-1-50-2 Henderson 16-5-41-1 Mongia 3-0-7-0

YORKSHIRE WON BY SIX WICKETS

Bibliography

John Arlott, *Fred – Portrait of a Fast Bowler*
Philip Bailey, Philip Thorn, Peter Wynne-Thomas: *Who's Who of Cricketers*
Jack Bannister: *The Innings of My Life*
Geoff Boycott: *The Autobiography*
Robert Brooke: *A History of the County Cricket Championship;*
       The Cricketer Book of Cricket Milestones
John Callaghan: *Yorkshire's Pride*
Brian Close: *I Don't Bruise Easily*
Ken Dalby: *White is the Rose – The Headingley Story Vol. 3: County Cricket*
Leslie Duckworth: *Holmes and Sutcliffe – the Run Stealers*
Paul Dyson: *Benson & Hedges Cup Record Book 1972-1995; Yorkshire's 30 Championships 1893-2001;*
       (with Mick Pope) *100 Greats – Yorkshire County Cricket Club*
Bill Frindall: *The Wisden Book of Test Cricket;*
       England Test Cricketers
David Frith: *Pageant of Cricket*
Ed. Benny Green: *Wisden Anthology 1864-1900; Wisden Anthology 1900-1940*
John Hampshire: *Family Argument*
Alan Hill: *A Chain of Spin Wizards;*
       Brian Close – Cricket's Lionheart;
       Hedley Verity – a Portrait of a Cricketer;
       Herbert Sutcliffe – Cricket Maestro
Rev. R.S. Holmes: *The History of Yorkshire County Cricket 1833-1903*
Gerald Howat: *Len Hutton – the Biography*
Richard Isaacs, Vic Isaacs:: *Gillette Cup/NatWest Trophy Record Book*
J.M. Kilburn: *A History of Yorkshire Cricket*
J. Ledbetter: *First-Class Cricket – A Complete Record 1930-39*
Don Mosey: *Fred – Then and Now*
Mick Pope: *Yorkshire CCC* (The Archive Photograph Series);
       Tragic White Roses
E.L. Roberts: *Yorkshire's 22 Championships 1893-1946*
Herbert Sutcliffe: *For Yorkshire and England*
Fred Trueman: *Ball of Fire; My Most Memorable Matches*
Roy Wilkinson: *Yorkshire County Cricket Club First-Class Records 1863-1996*
Tony Woodhouse: *The History of Yorkshire CCC; Yorkshire Cricketers 1863-1985*
Jason Woolgar: *England – the Complete One-Day International Record*
Peter Wynne-Thomas: *The Hamlyn A-Z of Cricket Records*
       The Complete History of Cricket Tours at Home and Abroad

ACS Publications including *Complete First-Class Match Lists, Counties Booklets, First-Class Match Scores*

Various editions of: *Birmingham Post, The Cricketer, James Lillywhite's Cricketers' Annual, Playfair Cricket Annual, Playfair Cricket Monthly, The Sheffield & Rotherham Advertiser, Sheffield Telegraph, The Times, Wisden Cricketers' Almanack, Wisden Cricket Monthly, Yorkshire CCC Year Book, Yorkshire Post*

Other local titles published by STADIA

Yorkshire CCC 100 Greats
MICK POPE AND PAUL DYSON

The County Championship is the greatest cricket competition in the world. The fact that Yorkshire, with 29 titles, is pre-eminent in its history suggests that its Broad Acres have produced many great players. From George Anderson, who first played for Yorkshire in 1850, through to Matthew Hoggard, who received the coveted county cap in 2000, this book features 100 of the cricketers who have shaped Yorkshire CCC.

978 07524 2179 7

Yorkshire County Cricket Club
MICK POPE

This book of over 200 photographs is a tribute to those who helped put Yorkshire in the forefront of the cricket world. It covers the club's history from the beginnings in Sheffield through the dominant years between the wars when Yorkshire won the County Championship on twelve occasions to the 1960s when another six Championship crowns and two domestic one-day titles came back to the county.

978 07524 0756 2

Herbert Sutcliffe Cricket Maestro
ALAN HILL

A national hero in his playing days, Herbert Sutcliffe belongs to a select band of all-time cricketing greats. This biography of the Yorkshire and England batsman charts his extraordinary transformation from cobbler's apprentice to urbane gentleman, and one of the coolest, most determined and technically accomplished practitioners the game has ever known.

978 07524 4350 8

If you are interested in purchasing other books published by Stadia, or in case you have difficulty finding any Stadia books in your local bookshop, you can also place orders directly through the Tempus website

www.tempus-publishing.com